# Ancient Book of

# Enoch

by
Ken Johnson, Th.D.

Ancient Book of Enoch
by Ken Johnson, Th.D.

Printed in the United States of America

ISBN 1480102768
EAN-13 978-1480102767

Unless otherwise indicated, Bible quotations are from the KJV. Chapter and verse divisions are based on the R. H. Charles edition.

# Contents

# Introduction

Enoch was the seventh generation from Adam, the first man God created (Genesis 5:1-24). From Scripture we know Enoch lived for 365 years and then was translated or raptured without dying, and that even though he was a sinner like every other human being, he pleased God with his lifestyle.

> And Enoch lived sixty and five years, and begat Methuselah: and Enoch walked with God after he begat Methuselah three hundred years, and begat sons and daughters: and all the days of Enoch were three hundred sixty and five years: and Enoch walked with God: and he *was* not; for God took him. *Genesis 5:21-24*

> By faith Enoch was translated that he should not see death; and was not found, because God had translated him: for before his translation he had this testimony, that he pleased God. But without faith it is impossible to please Him: for he that cometh to God must believe that He is, and that He is a rewarder of them that diligently seek Him.
> *Hebrews 11:5-6*

Enoch named his firstborn son Methuselah (Genesis 5:22). The name Methuselah is made up of two Hebrew words; "meth" meaning "death" and "selah" meaning "to send." The way Genesis 5:22 puts these two words together is unique. The spelling suggests the name can be translated as a Hebrew sentence meaning "when he is dead, it will be sent." If we add the years from creation to the birth of Methuselah as found in Genesis 5, and then add his age at death, we find he died the very same year the Flood came. If we look in the ancient book of Jasher 5:36, we see Methuselah died exactly one week before the Flood occurred. This is the same day Noah entered the Ark! (Genesis 7:1-4).

The timing clearly shows Enoch knew of the prophecy of God's judgment of the world and, apparently, God gave Enoch a prophecy that the day his son died would be the end of the world as he knew it! This would, indeed, keep Enoch centered on both his son and the teachings of God throughout his whole life, walking very closely with God.

Theologian John Gill (AD 1697-1771) wrote about the Book of Enoch saying:

> "Enoch, the seventh from Adam, delivered out the prophecy referred to by the apostle Jude, (verses 14, 15) ... the Jews make mention of a writing of his in their ancient book of Zohar; and in the Targum of Jonathan on Genesis 5:24, he is called the great scribe; and several of the Christian fathers speak of his book as authentic, as Tertullian and others; and the Arabic writers [Flavius Josephus] tell us of pyramids and pillars erected by him, on which he engraved the arts and the instruments of them; and

some writers ascribe the invention of letters and writing of books to him" *A Dissertation Concerning the Antiquity of the Hebrew Language, Letters, Vowel Points, and Accents, by John Gill, D.D., ch. 2, pg. 36*

## The Book of Enoch, 2800-200 BC

If the legends are to be believed, Enoch passed his book and other books to Noah, who preserved them in the Ark. Noah then passed Enoch's book on to Shem, who preserved it in the city of Salem. Eventually it was passed down to the Israeli tribe of Levi for safe keeping. Somewhere along the line a new Hebrew translation renamed some of the place names of the cities, rivers, and lands. This was most likely done around the time of Solomon. It was then preserved up to the time the Essenes buried it, along with other ancient texts, to be found among the Dead Sea Scrolls.

## The Ancient Church on Enoch, AD 32-700

The Book of Enoch is quoted by church fathers and rabbis alike, all the way back to the first century. By the year AD 700 it was forgotten by the church as a whole. Here are a few quotes from the ancient church fathers that let us know that the Ethiopic version of Enoch (called 1 Enoch) was considered the *real* Book of Enoch and that it contained *real* prophecy. It was not, however, to be added to the canon of Scripture, but was considered recommend reading by Scripture much like the *Ancient Book of Jasher*. What we know today as 2 Enoch and 3 Enoch were never considered real by either the church or the ancient rabbis.

Origen, *Of First Principles 4.1.35*, quotes Enoch 41 and 17.

Origen, *Against Celsus 5.48,54*, shows that Celsus' quote of Enoch's prophecy of seventy angels is from 2 Enoch. Origen corrects him by stating that the books of Enoch he was using (2 and 3 Enoch) are not received by Jews or Christians.

Irenaeus, *Against Heresies 4.16*, summarized the story of Enoch 6-16.

Tertullian, *On Idolatry 4*, said Enoch taught that the demons and spirits of the apostate angels turned everything pure into idolatry.

Anatolius 5 says the Book of Enoch clearly shows the Hebrew New Year begins about the time of the equinox.

Testament of Levi 10 teaches that the Book of Enoch says the Jews will be scattered among the heathen and the temple will be at Jerusalem.

Theodotus 2 quotes Enoch as saying "I have seen all sorts of matter."

Tertullian, *Apparel of Women 1.2*, summarized the errors taught by the fallen angels in Enoch 6-16.

Tertullian, *Apparel of Women 1.3*, says the Book of Enoch is genuine. The Book of Enoch was not received by some Christians because it was not part of the Jewish canon. The Jews [Pharisees] rejected it, like some portions of Scripture, because it testified of Christ. Its quotation from the epistle of Jude proves it is to be considered genuine prophecy.

Tertullian, *Treatise on the Soul 50*, says Enoch and Elijah will return to earth (his interpretation of Enoch 90:31). Tertullian, *Idolatry 1.4, 15*, quotes the Book of Enoch.

## AD 1768-1948

A man named James Bruce heard that the only translation known to still exist of the lost Book of Enoch was preserved by the Ethiopian Christian Church. In AD 1768, Bruce travelled to Ethiopia to find the Book of Enoch. Six years later, in 1773, he brought three manuscripts back to London where they lay in the British Museum untranslated. One hundred and twenty years later, in 1893, a man named R. H. Charles translated the manuscripts from the Ethiopic language into English.

### Liberal Scholarship

The Book of Enoch has been largely ignored by fundamentalist Christians. Most of the commentaries on the book have been liberal. The same people who declare the biblical book of Daniel to be a creation of the Maccabean period because its prophecy in chapter 11 is far too accurate to have been written in the fifth century BC, say the same thing concerning the Book of Enoch. Considering the Daniel 11 prophecy proves itself by predicting events beyond the Maccabean period up to the reestablishment of Israel in AD 1948, Bible-believing Christians need to take a second look at the Book of Enoch.

Liberals theorized that the current Book of Enoch was a compilation of five separate works, or that there have been at least five separate scribes who translated the present version. Most scholars divided Enoch into five sections.

| Section | Date | Chapters | Notes |
|---------|------|----------|-------|
| 1 | 200-150 BC | 1-36 | Book of Watchers |
| 2 | 1-100 AD* | 37-71 | Book of Parables |
| 3 | 200 BC | 72-82 | Book of Astronomy |
| 4 | 165-160 BC** | 83-90 | Book of Dreams and Visions |
| 5 | 150 BC | 91-108 | Epistle of Enoch |

* Late date based only on the fact it was not found in the Dead Sea Scrolls
** Thought to be composed during the Maccabean revolt.

The style of writing appears to be about 200 BC, which explains why some liberals would believe it is a collection of five separate fake works put together by non-intellectual people who still believe in prophecy like the biblical book of Daniel.

**Fundamentalist Scholarship**
Since we can see that editing was done, such as replacing the ancient names of cites and rivers (e.g. Dan and Mt. Hermon), then we know the current version of the Book of Enoch is a translation of the original. This means it may have errors in it; it may be wholly corrupted in some sections, but it may also contain real history and real prophecy relevant to our generation.

Fragments of the Book of Enoch were found among the Dead Sea Scrolls in both the Hebrew and Greek languages. Later, in AD 1956, a Dead Sea Scroll was found to contain the whole Book of Enoch written in Aramaic. When this Aramaic version is published, it will

9

prove the parables section was indeed pre-Christian and that the prophecies about the coming of the "Son of Man," or Messiah, were written before the Christian church began.

## Enoch Should Not Be Placed in the Scripture

The Book of Enoch teaches that the righteous are to live their lives by a series of books that will be given to them. Further, they will be judged by these books, not the Book of Enoch (104). Now we know this to be true; Christians are judged by the sixty-six books of the Bible. Because of the way Enoch states this, it is obvious that the Book of Enoch was not supposed to be placed into the canon of Scripture but kept as a special message to those who lived in the generation just prior to the Tribulation period.

## Conclusion

We have a translation of the real Book of Enoch which has been edited from time to time. The style of writing suggests this translation of Enoch was done about 1000 BC and possibly again in 200 BC. If we find that it contains accurate prophecy, we must see it as a true gift from God.

Look at these charts below to see Enoch's doctrines and prophecies and how they line up with Scripture.

| Biblical Phrases Quoted From Enoch | Enoch | Bible |
|---|---|---|
| Head and not the tail | 103:11 | Isa. 9:14 |
| Sinners will be weighed in the balances | 41:1 | Dan. 5:27 |
| God is no respecter of persons | 63:8 | Eph. 6:9 |
| It is better for sinners "if they were never born" | 38:2 | Mark 14:21 |
| We will be protected "under His wings" | 39:7 | Ps. 17:8 |

10

| Biblical Doctrines Found in Enoch | Enoch | Bible |
|---|---|---|
| No Flesh is righteous before the Lord | 81:5 | Rom. 3:10 |
| Abortion is murder | 98:5; 99:5 | Ex. 21:22-23 |
| God is omniscient and omnipotent | 9:5 | Jer. 23:24 |
| Flood covered the entire earth | 106:15 | Gen. 7:19 |
| Noah and family spent one year in the ark | 106:15 | Gen. 7:11;8:14 |
| Meditation (sorcery) blinds men to God | 99:8 | Rom. 1:21 |
| Denying inspiration is calling God a liar | 104:9 | 2 Tim. 3:16 |
| All pre-flood men and giants perished | 89:6 | Gen. 7:4 |
| Do not alter the Scripture | 104:9 | Rev. 22:18-19 |
| Ignoring prophecy is a serious sin | 108:6 | Luk. 24:25 |
| Book of Enoch not to be added to the Bible | 104 | Rev. 22:18 |

| Doctrines About the Messiah | Enoch | Bible |
|---|---|---|
| Messiah is the Son of God | 105:2 | 1 Jn. 5:5 |
| Salvation hangs on the Messiah | 40:5 | Acts 4:12 |
| Salvation by repentance and belief in His Name | 50:2-3 | Luk. 13:3 |
| Salvation by believing on the Messiah's name | 45:3; 48:7 | Acts 4:12 |
| Salvation is by the righteousness of faith | 39:6 | Rom. 4:11 |
| Messiah's name (Yeshua) is hinted at | 5:7 | Isa. 12:2-3 |
| Messiah is called the "Word" | 90:38 | Joh. 1:1 |
| The Messiah is called the Son of Man | 48:10 | Mat. 9:6 |
| Son of Man exists with God the Father eternally | 48:6 | 2 Sam. 7:14 |
| Messiah's shed blood is necessary for salvation | 47:2,4 | Mat. 26:28 |
| Son of Man existed before any created thing | 48:2-3, 6 | Ps. 102:25-27 |
| Messiah preserves the righteous | 48:7 | Jn. 17:12 |
| Messiah will be a light unto the nations | 48:4 | Isa. 42:6 |

| First Coming Prophecies | Enoch | Bible |
|---|---|---|
| Messiah born of a virgin | 62:5 | Isa. 7:14 |
| Jews will deny the Messiah | 48:10 | Joh. 1:11 |
| Elect One will resurrect from the dead | 51:5 | Joh. 21:14 |
| Bible given to the righteous | 104 | 2 Tim. 3:16 |
| The Righteous One will resurrect | 92:3 | Joh. 21:14 |
| The Righteous One will give eternal life | 5:9; 92:4 | Joh. 10:28 |
| Man errs respecting time and the calendar | 75:2, 82:5,9 | Luk. 19:44 |

| End Time Prophecies | Enoch | Bible |
|---|---|---|
| Angels will never crossbreed again | 68:5 | - |
| Corrupted Bibles will be created | 99,104 | Rev. 22:18-19 |
| Jude's quote of Enoch | 1:9 | Jud. 1:14-15 |
| Everyone will kneel before the Messiah | 48:5; 57:3 | Phil. 2:10 |
| Everyone will resurrect | 62:5 | Rev. 20:5 |
| Rapture is taking "out of the midst" | 70:2 | 2 Thes. 2:7 |
| "Valley of dry bones" mentioned | 90:4 | Ezek. 37:4 |
| Years will be shortened | 80:2 | Mat. 24:22 |
| The Rapture and Resurrection is a mystery | 103:2 | 1 Cor. 15:51 |
| Rapture before the Tribulation to cause repentance | 50:1-5 | Dan. 12:3 |
| Rapture mentioned as "the Mercy" | 1:8; 5:5 | Jud. 1:21 |
| Truth altered in the latter days | 104:10-13 | Rev. 22:18-19 |
| Iran will attack Israel, God sends confusion | 56:5-7 | Ezek. 38-39 |
| Days will be shortened | 80:2 | Mat. 24:22 |
| The Moon will change its order | 80:4 | Rev. 6:12-13 |
| There will be blood up to a horse's breast | 100:3 | Rev. 14:20 |
| Millennium mortals and immortals dwell together | 39:1 | Rev. 20:4 |
| There will be 7000 years of history | 93 | - |

The Book of Enoch opens by stating it was written to the generation of the Tribulation.

# The Book of Enoch

# End-Time Outline 1-5

## 1 The Time of Destruction

"These are the words of the blessing of Enoch, to bless the elect and righteous,[A] who will be living in the day of Tribulation, when all the wicked and godless will be destroyed. [2]God opened the eyes of the righteous Enoch, so that the angels could show him a vision of the Holy One in the heavens. 'From them I understood that the vision I saw was not for my generation, but for a far distant one.'

[3]On the account of the elect, the great Holy One, the God of the world, will come forth from His dwelling and [4]tread upon the earth,[B] appearing with His host in the strength of His might from the heavens.

[5]All will be afraid and the Watchers[C] will tremble. Great fear and trembling will seize everyone all over the whole earth. [6]The high mountains will be shaken, and the high hills will be brought low, melting like wax in a flame.[D]

---

[A] Jews are the elect of God. Christians are righteous by being justified in Christ.

[B] Most translations have "Mt. Sinai" rather than "the earth." This first section seems to be focused on the Second Coming of Christ, who is the "God of the world." The phrase "the earth" seems more accurate; unless Enoch is trying to tell us the fleeing Jews gather back at Mt. Sinai where the Law was given, instead of gathering at Petra as most prophecy teachers believe.

[C] Watchers are a class of angels, see Daniel 4:13.

[D] 2 Peter 3:7, 10

[7]The earth will be torn apart, and life on earth will perish. All men will be judged.

[8]However, He will make peace with them, protecting the elect, and showing the righteous *the Mercy*.[E] For they all belong to God, and will prosper and be blessed when they see Him at His appearing."

> "[9]Behold! He comes with ten thousands of His holy ones to execute judgment upon all, to destroy all the ungodly, to convict all flesh of all the works of their ungodliness which they have ungodly committed, and of all the harsh things which ungodly sinners have spoken against Him." *Quoted in Jude 14-15*

## 2 Observe Nature
"Observe how the stars in heaven do not change orbit but follow the proper paths rising and setting in their proper time without transgressing the commands they have received. [2]Observe the earth. Everything comes and goes in its season; nothing changes. [3]Summer is followed by winter again and again. The sun dries and the clouds dew, and rains replenish the whole earth.

## 3 
Observe how every autumn the leaves change color and fall, then are made anew in the spring, except

---

[E] Keep yourselves in the love of God, looking for the mercy of our Lord Jesus Christ unto eternal life. *Jude 1:21*- "the Mercy" is a term used in Scripture for the Rapture.

fourteen trees[F] which do not lose their leaves yearly but their leaves remain two or three years until the new leaves come.

4 Every summer you shelter yourself from the sun's heat because the rocks get so hot you cannot walk barefoot on them.

5 The trees sprout leaves and fruit every spring. Do you not understand that He who lives forever made these things for you? [2]All His works continue from year to year forever; they do not change. All of His tasks are accomplished because He has ordained them so. [3]Observe how the sea and rivers accomplish their purpose; they do not turn away from the paths that He has commanded them."

### The Ungodly

"[4]But you do not patiently endure trials, nor obey the commandments of the Lord; instead, you have turned away and spoken great and swelling words[G] with your impure mouths against His majesty. You hard-hearted ones will find no peace. [5]Your days will be shortened and your lives cursed! You will die and spend eternity in hell;

---

[F] Fourteen species of evergreens existed in the pre-flood world.

[G] These are murmurers, complainers, walking after their own lusts; and their mouth speaketh great swelling words, having men's persons in admiration because of advantage. *Jude 1:16*; For when they speak great swelling words of vanity, they allure through the lusts of the flesh, through much wantonness, those that were clean escaped from them who live in error. *2 Peter 2:18*

you will not obtain *the Mercy*.[H] [6]In those days you will give up your peace,[I] and not only the righteous, but the sinners and ungodly, will curse you.

## The Godly

[7]Salvation [Yeshua] will be for the elect, but not for the sinners. But the elect will inherit the earth[J] with light, joy, and peace. [8]Then wisdom will be given to the elect and they will live eternally and never sin again through ungodliness and pride. They will be humble and prudent. [9]They will not die in the time of wrath when their number is complete; but instead, live in peace with the number of their years multiplied eternally."

---

[H] Jude 21 - a Raptured, glorified body. "The Mercy" is a term for the Rapture in Scripture.

[I] For when they speak great swelling words of vanity, they allure through the lusts of the flesh, through much wantonness, those that were clean escaped from them who live in error. *2 Peter 2:18*

[J] Matthew 5:5; Psalm 1:1-6

# The Watchers 6-16

## 6 The Descent of the Two Hundred Angels

It came to pass in those days that the children of men multiplied and beautiful and fair daughters[A] were born unto them. [2]The angels, the sons of the heaven, saw and lusted after them, and said to one another, "Come, let us choose wives from among the children of men and beget children." [3]And their leader, Semyaza, said to them, "I am afraid that you will not truly agree to do this deed, and I alone will have to pay the penalty of this great sin." [4]They all answered him saying, "We should all swear to bind ourselves by a mutual oath not to abandon this plan, but to do this thing." [5]So all together they bound themselves by an oath. There were two hundred, total, that descended[B] in the days of Jared[C] upon Ardis, the summit of Mount Hermon.[D] [6]They called it Mount Hermon, because they had sworn and bound themselves by oath upon it. [7]These are the names of their leaders: Semyaza, their leader, Arakibal, Rameel, Akibeel, Tamiel, Ramuel, Danel, Ezeqeel, Barakel, Asael, Armaros, Batraal, Ananel,

---

[A] Genesis 6:1-2

[B] And the angels which kept not their first estate, but left their own habitation, he hath reserved in everlasting chains under darkness unto the judgment of the great day. *Jude 1:6*

[C] Between 460 and 622 AM (years after Creation).

[D] Mount Herman can be translated "sacred mountain," or "devoted to destruction." Joshua 12:5 records Mt. Herman as the place where the giant, Og, ruled.

Zavebe, Samsapeel, Satarel, Turel, Yomyael, Sariel. [8]These leaders led the rest of the two hundred angels.[E]

## 7 Giants Born

Each of the two hundred chose a wife for himself and they began to go in unto them and to mate with them, and they taught them sorcery[F] and enchantments, and the cutting of roots, and made them acquainted with plants. [2]These women became pregnant and gave birth to great giants[G], whose height reached up to three thousand ells[H]. [3]These giants consumed all the food; and when men could no longer sustain them, [4]the giants turned against them and devoured mankind. [5]They also began to sin against birds, and beasts, and reptiles, and fish, and to devour one another's flesh, and drink the blood.[I] [6]Then the earth laid accusation against the lawless ones.

## 8 Forbidden Teachings

Azazel taught men to make swords, knives, shields, and armor from the metals of the earth. He taught the women how to see behind them,[J] how to make bracelets, ornaments, and other kinds of jewelry using precious

---

[E] Compare this list of 19 to the 21 listed in Enoch 69

[F] See Deuteronomy 18:10-11 and *Ancient Paganism* pp. 59.

[G] Genesis 6:4-6

[H] This is probably a corruption of thirty. An ell was the equivalent of a Hebrew Cubit. So, thirty ells or cubits would be equal to between forty and forty-five feet. The tallest post-flood giant mentioned in Scripture was Og, king of Bashan, who was just short of thirteen feet tall.

[I] Matthew 24:37-39

[J] Mirrors

stones[K] and the beautifying of the eyes with makeup of various colors. [2]This led them astray into fornication and ungodliness and they became corrupt in all their ways.

[3]Semyaza taught enchantments, and root-cuttings.
Armaros taught how to resolve enchantments.
Barakel taught astrology.
Kokabel taught the constellations (signs).
Temel taught the knowledge of the clouds (astrology).
Asradel taught the courses of the moon.

[4]As mankind began to perish, they cried out to Heaven.

## 9 Holy Angels Ask God to Intervene

Then Michael, Gabriel, Raphael, and Uriel[L] looked down from heaven and saw all the bloodshed upon the earth by the extreme lawlessness. [2]They said one to another, "the earth is laid waste and the voice of all the dead cries up to the gate of heaven. [3]The souls of men cry out to the holy ones of heaven saying, 'bring our cause before the Most High.'" [4]They said to the Lord, the King, "Lord of lords, God of gods, and King of kings, the throne of Your glory endures throughout all the ages, and Your name is holy, glorious, and blessed unto all the ages! [5]You have made all things, and have power over all things, and You see all things; nothing is hidden from You. [6]You see what Azazel has done, teaching unrighteousness on earth and revealing the eternal secrets concealed in heaven. [7]Semyaza and those he has authority

---

[K] For earrings
[L] Raphael and Uriel or Surian and Urian

over have taught sorcery. [8]And they have defiled themselves by sleeping with the daughters of men and revealed to those women these kinds of sins. [9]These women have begotten giants, and by their children the whole earth has been filled with blood and unrighteousness. [10]Now the souls of the dead are crying out to the gates of heaven because of the lawlessness which has taken place on the earth. [11]You know all things before they come to pass.[M] You allow this, but have not told us what we should do to the giants who are destroying Your creation.

# 10 God Passes Judgment
Then the Most High, the Great and Holy One, said to Uriel, "Go to the son of Lamech [Noah], and [2]tell him in My name 'Hide thyself!' Reveal to him the judgment that is approaching: that all life will be destroyed by a flood of water that will cover the entire earth. [3]Instruct him how he may escape and his seed may be preserved throughout all the generations of the world.[N]"

## Azazel Ritual[O]
[4]The Lord said to Raphael, "bind Azazel hand and foot, and cast him into the darkness. Make an opening in the

---

[M] Known unto God are all his works from the beginning of the world. *Acts 15:18*

[N] Genesis 6:11-22

[O] This event is commemorated by the scapegoat ritual described in Leviticus 16. See *Ancient Messianic Festivals* pp. 97-100 for details.

desert, which is in Dudael[P], and bind him there. [5]And place upon him rough and jagged rocks, and cover him with darkness, and let him abide there forever, and cover his face that he may not see light. [6]And on the day of the great judgment, he will be cast into the fire. [7]And heal the earth which the angels have corrupted[Q], and proclaim the healing of the earth, that I will heal it, so that not all the children of men perish through all the secret things that the Watchers have disclosed and have taught their sons. [8]The whole earth has been corrupted through the works that were taught by Azazel, so ascribe all these sins to him."

[9]The Lord said to Gabriel, "Proceed against the bastards, the reprobates, against the children of fornication.[R] Destroy the children of fornication and the children of the Watchers from amongst men. Cause them to go forth against one another that they may destroy each other in battle, for they will not have long life. [10]Grant no request that their fathers may make to you on behalf of their

---

[P] This place is called Beit HaDudo in the Talmud. See *Ancient Messianic Festivals* pp. 97-100 for the complete study on this ritual of Yom Kippur.

[Q] For unto the angels hath he not put in subjection the world to come, *Hebrews 2:5*

[R] There were three clans of pre-flood giants - They begat sons, the Nâphîdîm, and they were all unlike, and they devoured one another: and the Giants slew the Nâphîl, and the Nâphîl slew the Eliô [Elioud], and the Eliô, mankind, and one man another. *Jubilees 7:22*

children; for they hope to live an eternal life; but none of them will live past five hundred years[S]."

## The Seventy Generations

[11]The Lord said to Michael, "Go, tell Semyaza and his associates who have defiled themselves by marrying women, that they and all those they contaminated will be destroyed. [12]When they have seen their sons slay one another and all their loved ones destroyed, bind them for seventy generations[T] under the valleys of the earth, until the day of their judgment and of their end, till their last judgment be passed for all eternity. [13]In those days they will be led off to the fiery abyss, to the torment and the prison in which they will be confined forever. And [14]whosoever was condemned and destroyed will from thenceforth be bound together with them to the end of all generations.[U] [15]Destroy all the spirits of the reprobate and the children of the Watchers, because they have oppressed mankind. [16]Destroy all wrong from the face of the earth and let every evil work come to an end:

---

[S] Within five hundred years of this prophecy, the giants fought in their civil war, which completely annihilated their race.

[T] According to Luke 3:23-38, there were seventy generations from Enoch to Jesus Christ. The miracles associated with the Azazel ritual preformed on Yom Kippur each year stopped when the Messiah died on the cross. See *Ancient Messianic Festivals* pp. 99, 119. Jesus made atonement and ascended to heaven. The fallen angels remained bound until the seventy generations passed and Christ completed His work. Now they await their last judgment, to be cast into the lake of fire.

[U] All those who joined Azazel were contaminated; their bodies were destroyed and burned completely by the holy angels. Today their spirits await the final judgment.

## Millennial Reign

and let the plant of righteousness and truth appear, and it will prove a blessing; the works of righteousness will be planted in truth and joy forevermore. [17]Then will all the righteous escape, and live till they could beget a thousand children.[V] All the days of their youth and old age will they complete in peace. [18]Then will the whole earth be tilled in righteousness, and will all be planted with trees and be full of blessing. [19]All desirable trees will be planted on it, and they will plant vines on it; and the vine which they plant will yield wine in abundance, and each seed which is sown will bear a thousand, and each measure of olives will yield ten presses of oil. [20]Cleanse the earth from all oppression, unrighteousness, sin, godlessness, and all the uncleanness that is wrought upon the earth destroy from off the earth. [21]Then all the children of men will become righteous, and all nations will worship Me, and will praise Me, and all will worship Me. [22]And the earth will be cleansed from all defilement, sin, punishment, and from all torment. I will never again send a flood of water upon it from generation to generation, forever.

11 In those days I will open the store chambers of blessing which are in the heavens, and send them down upon the earth over the work and labor of the children of men. [2]And truth and peace will be associated

---

[V] They would have to live to 1000 years old to be able to do this. This proverb is not saying they will beget, but that in the Millennial Reign they will live the same long life spans that existed before the Flood.

together throughout all the days of the world and throughout all the generations of men.

# 12 Enoch to Testify to the Angels

Enoch was hidden before all this came to pass. No one knew where he was or what he was doing. [2]At this time, his activities were with the Watchers and his days were spent with the holy ones.[W] [3]I, Enoch, was blessing the Lord, the King of the world, and suddenly the Watchers[X] called to me saying [4]"Enoch, scribe[Y] of righteousness, go to the fallen Watchers who have left the high heaven, the holy eternal place, and have defiled themselves with women, and have done as the children of earth do, and have taken unto themselves wives and greatly corrupted themselves on the earth; [5]tell them that they will not have peace nor forgiveness of sin, for they will not delight in their children. [6]They will witness the slaughter of their beloved ones, and will weep over the destruction of their children, and even if they petition for all eternity they will not obtain mercy or peace.[Z]"

---

[W] Genesis 5:21 states after he begat Methuselah, Enoch walked with God (Hebrew Elohim: God and/or angels) for his remaining 300 years.

[X] Holy angels, see Daniel 4:13-14

[Y] Legend holds that Enoch was the first scribe or the first to use writing.

[Z] For if God spared not the angels that sinned, but cast them down to hell, and delivered them into chains of darkness, to be reserved unto judgment; and spared not the old world, but saved Noah the eighth person, a preacher of righteousness, bringing in the flood upon the world of the ungodly; *2 Peter 2:4-5*

# 13 Enoch's Testimony to the Angels

Enoch went and said, "Azazel, you will not have peace; a severe sentence has gone forth against you and he[AA] will put you in bonds. [2]Your actions will not be tolerated nor will mercy be granted to you, because of your oppression and all the abuse, godlessness, and sin which you have taught to men."

[3]Then I went and spoke to them all together, and they were all afraid, and seized with fear and trembling. [4]They asked me to petition the Lord for them for forgiveness [5]because from this point on they could not speak with the Lord nor lift up their eyes toward heaven, ashamed on account of the shame of their sins for which they were condemned. [6]So I did as they asked and took their petition in regard to their individual deeds, forgiveness, and peace. [7]And I went off and sat down at the waters of Dan, in the land of Dan[BB], which is south of the land west of Mount Hermon. [8]I then fell asleep and dreamed about their chastisement and heard a voice instructing me to tell it to the sons of

---

[AA] The angel Raphael, see Enoch 10:4

[BB] The Ethiopic version is a translation of the original Hebrew. Therefore the names given here are the names for the mountains and lands in Bible times. The city of Dan is located just southwest of Mount Hermon. It is close by a stream that flows from the Lebanon Mountains and feeds the Jordan River. Senir was the Ammonite name for Mount Hermon. So the city Abelsiail could be between Mount Hermon and Lebanon and about the same distance to Dan as Mount Hermon is.

heaven, and reprimand them. [9]And when I awoke, I came unto them, and they were all sitting gathered together, weeping in Abelsiail (Ublesiael), which is between Lebanon and Seneser[CC], with their faces covered. [10]I recounted before them the dream, and I spoke words of righteousness, and reprimanded the fallen Watchers.

# 14 Judgment is Final

This is the record of the words of righteousness, and of the reprimand of the eternal Watchers I was commanded to give by the Holy Great One in that vision. [2]I will now relate what I saw in my dream with my tongue of flesh and the breath of my mouth that you may understand with your whole heart. [3]Just as He created man with the power of understanding the word of wisdom, He has created me and given me the power to reprimand the Watchers[DD], the children of heaven.

[4]I wrote out your petition, but in my vision I saw that your petition will not be granted unto you throughout all the days of eternity.[EE] Your judgment is final. [5]The decree is: from this point on you will be bound on earth throughout all the days of the world. You will not able to reenter heaven. [6]But before you are bound, you will see all your

---

[CC] An ancient rabbinic legend states that somewhere in what we call the mountains of Lebanon lies the ruins of the pre-flood city of Enoch built by Cain. Unfortunately, little or no archeology has ever been done in the Lebanese mountains.

[DD] Know ye not that we shall judge angels? *1 Corinthians 6:3*

[EE] And the angels which kept not their first estate, but left their own habitation, he hath reserved in everlasting chains under darkness unto the judgment of the great day. *Jude 1:6*

loved ones destroyed. You will not be able to possess them; you will only be able to watch them fall by the sword. [7]Your petition on their behalf, or for yourselves, will not be granted, even through you weep and pray. This I have written.

## The Dream of the Two Houses[FF]

[8]This was the vision that was shown to me: a mist enveloped me and a wind lifted me up to the clouds of heaven. I saw the stars and lightenings. [9]Then I was lifted up to heaven where I saw a wall made of crystals surrounded by tongues of fire that frightened me. [10]But I went through the tongues of fire[GG] and came to the crystal house. The walls and floor were made of interlaid crystals.[HH] [11]The ceiling was clear like water, but made up of swirling stars and lightenings with fiery cherubim in the midst of it. [12]A flaming fire surrounded the walls, and its door blazed with fire. [13]When I entered into that house, it was as hot as fire and as cold as ice. It was empty and there was nothing delightful in it, not even a trace of life. [14]I was so afraid I fell on my face and saw another vision.

[15]There appeared a second house, greater than the first, and all of its doors stood open before me, and it was built of flames of fire. [16]And in every respect it so excelled in splendor and magnificence to the extent that I cannot

---

[FF] The houses represent the two judgments: first, the water, then fire.
[GG] 2 Kings 2:11
[HH] Crystal sea - And before the throne there was a sea of glass like unto crystal: and in the midst of the throne, and round about the throne, were four beasts full of eyes before and behind. *Revelation 4:6*

describe to you. [17]And its floor was of fire, and above it were lightnings and the path of the stars, and its ceiling also was flaming fire. [18]Inside was a lofty throne made of hoarfrost with wheels shining as bright as the sun, and I heard the voices of the cherubim. [19]Streams of flaming fire flowed from underneath the throne so brightly I could not look directly at them.[II]

[20]The Great Lord sat upon this throne and His raiment was brighter than the sun and was whiter than any snow. [21]None of the angels could enter or could behold His face by reason of the magnificence and glory and no flesh could behold Him.[JJ] [22]The flaming fire was all around Him, and a great fire stood before Him, and none could come close to Him: ten thousand times ten thousand[KK] stood before Him, yet He needed no counselor. [23]And the most holy ones who were around Him never departed from Him, day or night.

[24]Until then I had a veil on my face, trembling; and the Lord called me with His own voice, and said to me,

---

[II] I beheld till the thrones were cast down, and the Ancient of Days did sit, whose garment was white as snow, and the hair of his head like the pure wool: his throne was like the fiery flame, and his wheels as burning fire. *Daniel 7:9*

[JJ] No man hath seen God at any time; the only begotten Son, which is in the bosom of the Father, he hath declared him. *John 1:18*

[KK] And I beheld, and I heard the voice of many angels round about the throne and the beasts and the elders: and the number of them was ten thousand times ten thousand, and thousands of thousands; saying with a loud voice, Worthy is the Lamb that was slain to receive power, and riches, and wisdom, and strength, and honour, and glory, and blessing. *Revelation 5:11-12*

"Come here, Enoch, and hear My word." [25]And one of the holy ones came to me and lifted me up to the door, and I bowed my face downwards.

## 15 The Judgment of the Ancient of Days

He said, "Fear not, Enoch, righteous man, and scribe of righteousness. [2]Go, say to the Watchers of heaven, who have sent you to intercede for them, 'You should intercede for men, and not men for you.' [3]Why have you left the eternal heaven, and lain with women, and defiled yourselves with the daughters of men by taking them as wives, like the children of earth do, and begotten giants as your sons? [4]Althrough you were holy, spiritual, living an eternal life, you have defiled yourselves with the blood of women, and have begotten children with the blood of flesh, and have lusted after flesh and blood as the children of men do who die and perish. [5]This is why I gave them wives, that they might beget children by them, so that nothing might be wanting to them on earth. [6]But you were formerly spiritual, immortal for all generations of the world, [7]which is why I did not appoint wives for you[LL]; for spiritual beings have heaven as their dwelling.

---

[LL] And Jesus answering said unto them, The children of this world marry, and are given in marriage: But they which shall be accounted worthy to obtain that world, and the resurrection from the dead, neither marry, nor are given in marriage: neither can they die any more: for they are equal unto the angels; and are the children of God, being the children of the resurrection. *Luke 20:34-36*

## Origin of Demons

[8]My judgment for the giants is that since they are born from flesh they will be called evil spirits and will remain on the earth. [9]Because they were created from above, from the holy Watchers, at death their spirits will come forth from their bodies and dwell on the earth. They will be called evil spirits. [10]The heavenly spirits will dwell in heaven, but the terrestrial spirits who were born on earth will dwell on earth. [MM] [11]The evil spirits of the giants will be like clouds. They will afflict, corrupt, tempt, battle, work destruction on the earth, and do evil; they will not eat nor drink, but be invisible. [12]They will rise up against the children of men and against the women, because they have proceeded from them.

16 When the giants die and their spirits leave their bodies, their flesh will decay without judgment. In this way the race will cease to exist until the great judgment in which the age will be wholly consummated over the Watchers and the godless.

[2]Now tell the fallen Watchers who have sent you to intercede for them, "[3]You were in heaven, but did not learn all the mysteries, just the worthless ones, and these, in your hard-heartedness, you have taught to the women and through these mysteries women and men produced

---

[MM] All flesh is not the same flesh: but there is one kind of flesh of men, another flesh of beasts, another of fishes, and another of birds. There are also celestial bodies, and bodies terrestrial: but the glory of the celestial is one, and the glory of the terrestrial is another. *1 Corinthians 15:39-40*

31

much evil on earth." [4]Therefore tell them, "You will not obtain peace!"

# Enoch's Journeys 17-36

## 17 Enoch's Travels

The angels took me to a place in which those who were there were like flaming fire, and, when they wished, they appeared as men.[A]

[2]Then they brought me to the place of darkness [whirlwind] and to a mountain the point of whose summit reached to heaven. [3]I saw the places of the luminaries and stars, the thunder, and in the uttermost depths, where was a fiery bow with arrows and a quiver, a fiery sword and all the lightnings.

[4]Then they took me to the living waters[B], and to the fire of the west, which receives every setting of the sun. [5]And I came to a river of fire[C] in which the fire flows like water and discharges itself into the great sea towards the west. [6]I saw the great rivers and came to the great river and to the great darkness, and went to the place where no flesh walks. [7]I saw the mountains of the darkness of winter and the place whence all the waters of the deep flow.[D] [8]I saw the mouths of all the rivers of the earth and the mouth of the deep.

---

[A] Seraphim, Isaiah 6:2
[B] Fresh water? Or constellation Pisces?
[C] Pacific Ring of Fire or Eridanus, the constellation of the River of Fire.
[D] Snow capped mountains where rivers begin

**18** I saw the chambers of all the winds, I saw how He had furnished the whole creation and the firm foundations of the earth with them. [2]I saw the cornerstone[E] of the earth. I saw the four winds which support the earth and the firmament of the heaven. [3]I saw how the winds stretch out the vaults of heaven, and have their station between heaven and earth; these are the pillars of the heaven.[F] [4]I saw the winds of heaven which turn and lead the course of the sun and all the stars.[G] [5]I saw the winds upon the earth which carry the clouds; I saw the paths of the angels. I saw at the end of the earth the firmament of the heavens above. [6]I proceeded and saw a place which burns day and night, where there are seven mountains of magnificent stones, three towards the east, and three towards the south. [7]As for those towards the east, one was of colored stone, and one of pearl, and one of jacinth, and those towards the south of red stone. [8]But the middle one reached to heaven like the throne of God, of alabaster, and the summit of the throne was of sapphire. [9]I saw a flaming fire over all the mountains. [10]Beyond these mountains is the region of the end of the great earth; there the waters collected.

[11]I saw a deep abyss, with columns of heavenly fire, and among them I saw columns of fire fall, which were beyond measure alike towards the height and towards the depth. [12]Beyond that abyss I saw a place which had no firmament of the heaven above, and no firmly founded

---

[E] Job 38:6; My guess is the Temple Mount in Jerusalem.
[F] How the mountains and rains form wind patterns over the earth
[G] The paths of the planets

earth beneath it; there was no water upon it, and no birds, but it was a waste and horrible place.

## The Seven Stars

[13] I saw there seven stars like great burning mountains, and like the spirits that petitioned me. When I inquired regarding them, [14] the angel said, "This place is the end of heaven and earth. This has become a prison for the stars and the host of heaven. [15] The stars which roll over the fire are those who transgressed the commandment of the Lord in the beginning of their rising because they did not come forth at their appointed times. [16] He was angry with them, and bound them till the time when their guilt should be consummated, in the year of mystery."

**19** Uriel said to me, "Here will stand the angels who have joined themselves with women. Their spirits appeared in various forms and defiled mankind by leading them astray into sacrificing to demons as gods. They will remain here until the day of great judgment when they will be judged and made an end of. [2] The fallen angels' wives will be with them."[H]

[3] I, Enoch, alone saw the vision, the end of all things, and no man will see these things as I have seen them.

**20** The Seven Holy Watchers
These are the names of the holy angels who

---

[H] Or "be their friends"

watch: [2]Uriel, who watches over thunder and terror[I]; Raphael, who watches over the spirits of men[J]; [3]Raguel, who takes vengeance on the earth and the luminaries; [4]Michael, who is set over the best part of mankind and the people[K]; [6]Saraqael, who is set over the spirits who sin[L]; [7]Gabriel,[M] who is over Paradise and the serpents[N] and the Cherubim; and Remiel, whom God set over those who rise.

# 21

Then I proceeded to a place where nothing was completed. [2]I saw there something horrible, a place with neither heaven nor earth, but an awful, terrible void. [3]There, seven stars of the heaven were bound together in it, like great mountains and burning with fire. [4]Then I exclaimed, "For what sin are they bound here?" [5]Then Uriel, who was with me, and was chief over them, said, "Enoch, why do you ask, and why are you so anxious? [6]These are the stars of heaven which have transgressed the commandment of the Lord, and are bound here till ten thousand worlds[O], the time entailed by their sins, are consummated."

[7]From there I went to another place which was still more horrible than the former. There I saw a great blazing fire,

---

[I] Over the weather of earth

[J] Records our prayers

[K] And at that time shall Michael stand up, the great prince which standeth for the children of thy people: *Daniel 12:1*

[L] Keeps in check the evil spirits who cause men to sin

[M] And the angel answering said unto him, I am Gabriel, that stand in the presence of God; *Luke 1:19*

[N] Or Seraphim

[O] "ten thousand worlds" probably means an infinite amount of time

and the place was divided and went down as far as the abyss. It was full of great descending columns of fire. I could not even guess how far down they went. [8]Then I said, "How fearful is the place and how terrible to look upon!"

[9]Then Uriel said to me, "Enoch, why are *you* so afraid of this terrible place of pain?" [10]He said unto me, "This place is the prison of the angels, and here they will be imprisoned forever."

## 22 Three Compartments of Hades / Sheol

From there I went to another place, and he showed me in the west a great and high mountain chain and of hard rocks and four beautiful places. [2]Beneath them were [three] deep, wide, and very smooth places, as smooth as if it were rolled over, and deep and dark to look upon.

[3]Then Raphael, one of the holy angels who was with me, answered, and said unto me: "These beautiful places have been created for this very purpose, that the spirits, the souls of the dead, should assemble in them.[P] [4]And these places have been made to receive them till the day of their judgment and till their appointed period (this period is long), till the great judgment comes upon them."

---

[P] Marvel not at this: for the hour is coming, in the which all that are in the graves shall hear his voice, and shall come forth; they that have done good, unto the resurrection of life; and they that have done evil, unto the resurrection of damnation. *John 5:28-29*

[5]I saw the spirits of the children of men who had died, and their voices went forth to heaven and made suit. [6]I asked the angel Raphael who was with me, and said unto him, "Whose spirit is that one whose voice goes forth and makes suit to heaven?"

[7]And he answered me saying, "This is the spirit which went forth from Abel, whom his brother Cain murdered[Q], and he makes his suit against him till his seed is destroyed from the face of the earth, and his seed is annihilated from amongst the seed of men."

[8]Then I asked regarding him and all the hollow places, "Why is one separated from the other?"

[9]He answered and said unto me, "These three places[R] have been made that the spirits of the dead might be separated. In this way, the spirits of the righteous are separated, in which there is the bright spring of water and a light about it. [10]One place was made for sinners when they die, and are buried in the earth and judgment has not been passed on them in their lifetime. [11]Here their spirits will be set apart in this great affliction till the great Day of Judgment and punishment and torment of revilers forever, and retribution for their spirits, and there He will bind them forever.[12]This place was made for the spirits of

---

[Q] Cain and Abel; see Genesis 4:10

[R] One place where the righteous dwell (Abrahams' Bosom - Luke 16:20-31), a second place where sinners dwell (the rich man), and a third place for the criminals or fallen angels and their wives and children (Tartarus - 2 Peter 2:4)

those who make their suit, who cry out concerning their destruction, when they were killed in the days of the sinners. [13]This was made for the spirits of men who were not righteous, but sinners, who were complete in crimes, and they will be with criminals like themselves; but their spirits will not be slain in the Day of Judgment nor will they be raised from there."

[14]Then I blessed the Lord of glory and said, "Blessed be my Lord, the Lord of Righteousness, who rules forever."

## 23 Sunset?

From there I went to another place to the west of the ends of the earth. [2]And I saw a burning fire which ran without resting, and paused not from its course day or night, but continued regularly. [3]And I asked saying, "What is this which does not rest?" [4]Then Raguel, one of the holy angels who was with me, answered me and said unto me, "This burning fire which you have seen running toward the west is the fire of all the luminaries of heaven."

## 24

From there I went to another place of the earth, and he showed me a mountain range of fire which burnt day and night.[S] [2]And I went beyond it and saw seven magnificent mountains[T] all differing from each other, and magnificent and beautiful stones, everything

---

[S] Volcanoes

[T] And I turned, and lifted up mine eyes, and looked, and, behold, there came four chariots out from between two mountains; and the mountains were mountains of brass. *Zechariah 6:1*

magnificent and fine in appearance with a beautiful surface; three towards the east, one founded on the other, and three towards the south, one upon the other, and deep rough ravines, no one of which joined with any other. [3]And the seventh mountain was between these, and it excelled them in height, resembling the seat of a throne, and fragrant trees surrounded it. [4]Among them was a tree such as I had never yet smelt, neither among these nor the others, it had a fragrance beyond all fragrance, and its leaves, blooms, and wood do not wither throughout all eternity; its fruit is beautiful, like the fruit of the vine and the palm tree.

[5]Then I said, "How beautiful and fragrant is this tree, and its leaves are fair and its blooms very pleasant to the eye."

[6]Then answered Michael, one of the holy and honored angels who was with me, who was over them.

# 25 Tree of Life[U]

He said unto me, "Enoch, why do you ask me regarding the fragrance of the tree, and why do you wish know?"

[2]Then I answered him saying, "I wish to know about everything, but especially about this tree."

---

[U] Tree of Life - Blessed are they that do his commandments, that they may have right to the tree of life, and may enter in through the gates into the city. *Revelation 22:14*

[3]And he answered saying, "This high mountain which you have seen, whose summit is like the throne of God, is His throne, where the Holy Great One, the Lord of Glory, the Eternal King, will sit when He will come down to visit the earth with goodness. [4]This fragrant tree (no mortal is permitted to touch it till the time of the Great Judgment, when all evil will be punished and consumed forever) will then be given to the righteous and humble. [5]Its fruit will be for food to the elect; it will be transplanted to the north in the holy place, to the temple of the Lord, the Eternal King. [6]Then they will greatly rejoice in the Holy One. Its fragrance will be in their bones, and they will live a long life on earth, like your fathers lived; in their days no sorrow, plague, torment, or affliction will touch them."

[7]Then I blessed the God of Glory, the Eternal King, who has prepared such things for the righteous, and has created them and promised to give to them.[V]

# 26 Land of Israel

[1]I went from there to the middle of the earth [Jerusalem], and I saw a blessed and fruitful place in which there were branches abiding in, and blooming from, a cut off tree.[W] [2]There I saw a holy mountain [Temple Mount], and underneath the mountain to the east

---

[V] In the midst of the street of it, and on either side of the river, was there the tree of life, which bare twelve manner of fruits, and yielded her fruit every month: and the leaves of the tree were for the healing of the nations. *Revelation 22:2*

[W] Jerusalem, where the Messiah died and resurrected to give us eternal life.

there was a stream and it flowed towards the south.[X] [3]I saw towards the east another mountain of the same height [Mount of Olives], and between them a deep and narrow valley [Kedron Valley], in it also ran a stream underneath the mountain. [4]Toward the west there was another mountain [upper city of Jerusalem], lower than the former and of small elevation, and a valley [Tyropoean Valley] between them, and another deep and sterile valley [Valley of Hinnom] was at the end of the three mountains. [5]All the valleys were deep and narrow, formed of hard rock, and trees were not planted upon them. [6]I marveled at the rocks, and at that valley; and I marveled very much.

# 27 Gehenna

Then I said, "For what purpose is this blessed land [Israel], which is entirely filled with trees, and this accursed valley between them?"

[2]Then Uriel, one of the holy angels who was with me, answered saying, "This cursed valley [Hinnom[Y]] is for those who will be cursed forever. Here will all the cursed be gathered together who utter with their lips unseemly words against the Lord and speak insolently of His glory. Here will they be gathered together, and here will be their place of judgment. [3]In the last days there will be upon them the spectacle of righteous judgment in the presence of the righteous forever. Here those who have found mercy will bless the Lord of Glory, the Eternal King. [4]In the days of judgment over the former, they will bless Him

---

[X] Stream that flows into the pool of Siloam.
[Y] Joshua 15:8; the valley of Hinnom, also called the Valley of Giants

for His mercy in accordance with which He has assigned to them." [5]Then I blessed the Lord of Glory and spoke to Him, and honored His glory, as was fitting.

## 28 Arabian Pre-Flood Rain Forest
From there I went toward the east, into the midst of the mountain range of the desert, and I saw a plain. [2]It was full of trees of this seed and water gushed forth from above. [3]A strong stream flowed toward the north and toward the west. It caused clouds and dew to ascend on every side.

## 29 Arabia and India
From there I went to another place away from the desert and approached to the east of this mountain range. [2]There I saw trees of judgment giving off the fragrance of frankincense and myrrh[Z], and the trees were not like ordinary trees. [3]These trees were right under the highest point in the eastern mountain range.

## 30 
Beyond these, I went far way[AA] to the east, and I saw another place, a valley full of water that does not dry up[BB]. [2]In there was a beautiful tree, its fragrance was such as the mastic[CC]. [3]On the sides of those valleys I saw fragrant cinnamon. Then I proceeded beyond these to the east.

---

[Z] Biblically these trees were abundant from Arabia to India
[AA] Or "not far away"
[BB] "Water that does not dry up" could be the Persian Gulf or Indian Ocean
[CC] Mastic is from the Mediterranean region.

# 31

I saw other mountains, and among them were groves of trees, and there flowed forth from them nectar, which is called storax and galbanum. ²Beyond these mountains I saw another mountain to the east of the ends of the earth, whereon were aloe trees, and all the trees were full of a hard substance, being like almond trees. ³When one burned it, it smelled sweeter than any fragrant odor.

# 32 Garden of Eden[DD]

After these fragrant odors, as I looked toward the north over the mountains, I saw seven mountains full of choice nard, fragrant trees, cinnamon, and pepper. ²From there I went over the summits of all these mountains, far towards the east of the earth, and passed above the Erythraean sea[EE] and went far from it, and passed over the angel Zotiel. ³And I came to the Garden of Righteousness [Eden]. I saw from afar off trees more numerous than these trees and two great trees there, very beautiful, glorious, and magnificent. The tree of knowledge, whose holy fruit they ate and knew great wisdom. ⁴That tree is in height like the fir, and its leaves are like the carob tree, and its fruit is like grapes, very beautiful, and the fragrance of the tree penetrates afar. ⁵Then I said, "How beautiful is the tree, and how glorious to look upon!"

⁶Then the holy angel Raphael, who was with me, answered me and said, "This is the tree of wisdom, of

---

[DD] The Garden of Eden would be at the north tip of the Persian Gulf; see *Ancient Post-Flood History* pp. 38-40 for details and a map.
[EE] Indian Ocean?

which your old father and your aged mother [Adam and Eve], who were before you, have eaten, and they learned wisdom and their eyes were opened, and they knew that they were naked and they were driven out of the garden."

# 33 The Constellations[FF]

From there I went to the ends of the earth and saw great beasts[GG] there, and each differed from the other; and I saw birds also differing in appearance and beauty and voice, the one differing from the other. [2]To the east of those beasts I saw the ends of the earth whereon the heaven rests, and the constellations of the heaven open. [3]I saw how the stars of heaven [sun and moon] come forth; and I counted the constellations out of which they proceed, and wrote down all their gates, of each individual star by itself, according to their number and their names, their courses and positions, and their times and months, as Uriel the holy angel who was with me showed me. [4]He showed me all these things and wrote them all down for me: their names, laws, and operations.[HH]

# 34 Seasonal Winds and Storms[II]

From there I went toward the north to the ends of

---

[FF] Anciently the stars and constellations had names. This gives credibility to the concept of the gospel in the stars. The information Uriel gave Enoch is the Astronomical Calendar section of this book.

[GG] Possibly the woolly mammoths of Siberia?

[HH] The information Uriel gave Enoch is the Astronomical Calendar section of this book.

[II] Weather patterns for seasons (the sun is in particular constellations).

the earth, and there I saw a great and glorious wonder at the ends of the whole earth. ²There I saw three portals of heaven open in the heaven; through each of them proceed north winds: when they blow there is cold, hail, frost, snow, dew, and rain. ³Out of one portal they blow for good; but when they blow through the other two portals, it is with violence and affliction on the earth, and they blow with violence.

**35** From there I went toward the west, to the ends of the earth, and saw there three open portals as I had seen in the east, the same number of portals, and the same number of outlets.

**36** Southern Hemisphere
From there I went to the south to the ends of the earth, and saw there three open portals of the heaven: out of them come dew, rain, and wind. ²From there I went to the east to the ends of the heaven, and saw here the three eastern portals of heaven open, and small portals above them. ³Through each one of these small portals pass the stars of heaven and run their course to the west on the path which is given to them. ⁴And as often as I saw, I blessed always the Lord of Glory, and I continued to bless the Lord of Glory who has wrought great and glorious wonders, to show the greatness of His work to the angels and to spirits of men, that they might praise His work and all His creation, that they might see the work of His might and praise the great work of His hands and bless Him forever.

**37** This is the second vision of wisdom of Enoch, son of Jared, son of Mahalalel, son of Cainan, son of Enos, son of Seth, son of Adam. [2]The very first words of wisdom from the Holy One that I wish to tell to those who dwell on earth, the men of old time[JJ] and those who will come after. [3]It would be better to declare it only to the men of old time, but I will not withhold wisdom from those who come after. [4]Never before has the Lord of Spirits given such wisdom. He also gave me my insight and eternal life. [5]The Lord of Spirits gave me three parables to tell to those who dwell on the earth.

---

[JJ] All the men from Adam to Enoch's time.

# First Parable 38-44

## 38 The First Parable.

When the congregation of the righteous will appear, sinners will be judged for their sins, and will be driven from the face of the earth. [2]And when the Righteous One [the Messiah] will appear before the eyes of the righteous and elect[A], whose works hang upon the Lord of Spirits[B], and light will appear to the righteous and the elect who dwell on the earth, — where then will be the dwelling of the sinners, and where the resting-place of those who have denied the Lord of Spirits? It would be better for them if they had not been born.[C] [3]When the secrets of the righteous will be revealed and the sinners judged, and the godless driven from the presence of the righteous and elect, [4]from that time those who possess the earth will no longer be powerful and exalted, nor will they be able to behold the face of the holy, for the Lord of Spirits has caused His light to appear on the face of the holy[D], righteous, and elect. [5]Then the mighty kings will perish, and be given into the hands of the righteous and holy. [6]From that time, none will be able to ask for mercy from the Lord of Spirits, for their life is at an end.[E]

---

[A] Righteous Christians and elect Jews

[B] Justified in Christ

[C] The Son of man goeth as it is written of Him: but woe unto that man by whom the Son of man is betrayed! It had been good for that man if he had not been born. *Matthew 26:24*

[D] Glorified bodies

[E] No chance of repentance or salvation after death.

**39** It will come to pass in those days, that elect and holy children will descend from the high heaven, and their seed will become one with the children of men.[F] [2]And in those days Enoch received books of zeal and wrath, of disturbance and expulsion,[G] and "mercy will not be granted to them," says the Lord of Spirits.

[3]And in those days a whirlwind carried me off from the earth, and set me down at the end of the heavens. [4]There I saw another vision, the dwelling-places of the holy and the righteous. [5]Here my eyes saw their dwellings with His righteous angels and the holy. And they asked, interceded, and prayed for the children of men, and righteousness flowed before them like water, and mercy like dew upon the earth. Thus it is among them forever. [6]In that place mine eyes saw the Elect One of righteousness of faith[H], and this righteousness will prevail in His days, and the righteous and elect will be without number before Him forever. [7]And I saw their dwelling-place under the wings[I] of the Lord of Spirits, and all the righteous and elect before Him will shine as fiery lights[J], and their mouth will

---

[F] In the Millennium, mortals and immortals will dwell together

[G] Great white throne judgment. - And I saw the dead, small and great, stand before God; and the books were opened: and another book was opened, which is the book of life: and the dead were judged out of those things which were written in the books, according to their works. *Revelation 20:12*

[H] For the promise, that he should be the heir of the world, was not to Abraham, or to his seed, through the law, but through the righteousness of faith. *Romans 4:13*

[I] He shall cover thee with His feathers, and under His wings shalt thou trust: *Psalms 91:4*

[J] Completely pure and clothed with light. See Daniel 12:3

be full of blessing, and their lips praise the name of the Lord of Spirits, and righteousness before Him will never cease. [8]There I wished to dwell, and my spirit longed for that dwelling-place, before this was my portion, for so has it been established concerning me before the Lord of Spirits.

[9]In those days I praised and extolled the name of the Lord of Spirits with blessings and praises, because He has destined me for blessing and glory according to the good pleasure of the Lord of Spirits.

[10]For a long time my eyes regarded that place, and I blessed and praised Him, saying, "Blessed is He, and may He be blessed from the beginning and forever. [11]And before Him there is no ceasing. He knew before the world was created what the world is, and what will be from generation unto generation. [12]Those who praise You do not sleep; they stand before Your glory and bless, praise, and exalt You, saying, 'Holy, holy, holy, is the Lord of Spirits; He fills the earth with spirits.[K]'" [13]Here my eyes saw all those who do not sleep. They stand before Him and bless Him, saying, "Blessed are You, and blessed is the name of the Lord forever.[L]" And my face was changed until I could see no more.

---

[K] And the four beasts had each of them six wings about him; and they were full of eyes within: and they rest not day and night, saying, Holy, holy, holy, Lord God Almighty, which was, and is, and is to come. *Revelation 4:8*

[L] And every creature which is in heaven... heard I saying, Blessing, and honour, and glory, and power, be unto him that sitteth upon the throne, and unto the Lamb for ever and ever. *Revelation 5:13*

# 40 The Four Archangels

And after that I saw thousands of thousands and ten thousand times ten thousand;[M] I saw a multitude beyond number, who stood before the Lord of Spirits. [2]And on the four sides of the Lord of Spirits I saw four beings, different from those that stood before Him, and I learned their names: for the angel that went with me told me their names, and showed me all the secrets. [3]And I heard the voices of those four beings as they uttered praises before the Lord of Glory. [4]The first voice blessed the Lord of Spirits forever. [5]And the second voice I heard blessing the Elect One and the elect ones[N] who hang[O] upon the Lord of Spirits. [6]And the third voice I heard asking and praying for those who dwell on the earth and interceding in the name of the Lord of Spirits. [7]And I heard the fourth voice fending off the adversaries[P] and forbidding them to come before the Lord of Spirits to accuse those who dwell on the earth.

[8]After that I asked the angel of peace who went with me, who showed me everything that is secret, "Who are these four beings which I have seen and whose words I have heard and written down?"

---

[M] And I beheld, and I heard the voice of many angels round about the throne and the beasts and the elders: and the number of them was ten thousand times ten thousand, and thousands of thousands; *Revelation 5:11*

[N] The Messiah and those who believe on Him.

[O] Their salvation hangs on the Messiah

[P] Literally "the satans"

[9]And he said to me, "This first is Michael[Q], the merciful and slow to anger; and the second, who is over all the diseases and wounds of the children of men, is Raphael; and the third, who is over all the powers, is Gabriel;[R] and the fourth, who is over the repentance and the hope of those who inherit eternal life, is Phanuel.[S]" [10]And these are the four angels of the Most High God and the four voices I heard in those days.

# 41

After that I saw all the secrets of the heavens, and how the kingdom is divided, and how the actions of men are weighed in the balance.[T] [2]And there I saw the mansions of the elect and the holy, and my eyes saw how all the sinners being driven away from there, those who deny the name[U] of the Lord of Spirits, are dragged off where there is no rest because of the punishment which proceeds from the Lord of Spirits.

[3]And there mine eyes saw the secrets of the lightning and thunder, and how the winds divide to blow over the earth, and the secrets of the clouds and dew, from where they proceed and how they saturate the dust of the earth. [4]And there I saw closed chambers out of which the winds are divided, and the chambers of the hail, mist, and clouds,

---

[Q] And at that time shall Michael stand up, the great prince which standeth for the children of thy people... *Daniel 12:1*

[R] And in the sixth month the angel Gabriel was sent from God unto a city of Galilee, named Nazareth, *Luke 1:26*

[S] And Jacob called the name of the place Peniel: for I have seen God face to face, and my life is preserved. *Genesis 32:30*

[T] TEKEL; Thou art weighed in the balances, and art found wanting. *Daniel 5:27*

[U] Yeshua or Jesus the Messiah.

First Parable

and of the cloud[V] that has covered the entire earth since the beginning of the world. [5]And I saw the chambers of the sun and moon, from where they proceed and where they come again, and their glorious return, and how one is superior to the other, and their fixed course, and how they do not leave their orbit, and they add nothing to their orbit and they take nothing from it, and they keep fidelity with each other, in accordance with the oath by which they are bound together. [6]And first the sun goes forth and follows the path that the Lord of Spirits has commanded, and mighty is His name forever. [7]And after that I saw the hidden and the visible course of the moon, and it accomplishes its course by day and by night — both holding their positions before the Lord of Spirits. By this they glorify Him and do not rest; for unto them their glorying is rest. [8]For the sun changes often for a blessing or a curse, and the course of the moon is light to the righteous and darkness to the sinners in the name of the Lord, who created separation between the light and the darkness, and divided the spirits of men, and strengthened the spirits of the righteous, in the name of His righteousness. [9]For no angel hinders and no power is able to hinder; for He sees them all and He judges them all before Him.

42 Wisdom found no place where she might dwell; so she was given a dwelling-place in the heavens. [2]Wisdom came to make her dwelling among the children of men, but found no dwelling-place. Wisdom returned to

---

[V] The pre-flood canopy.

her place, and took her seat among the angels. [3]Unrighteousness came forth from its chambers. Whom it did not seek, it found, and dwelt with them, like the rain in a desert and dew on a thirsty land.[W]

**43** Again I saw other lightnings and the stars of heaven, and I saw how He called them all by their names and they heard Him. [2]I saw how they are weighed on just scales according to their proportions of light, the width of their spaces[X], and the day of their appearing. I saw how one flash of lightening[Y] produces another, and their revolutions are according to the number of the angels, and how they keep fidelity with each other. [3]I asked the angel who went with me who showed me what was secret, "What are these?"

[4]And he said to me, "The Lord of Spirits has showed you their picture.[Z] These are the names of the holy who dwell on the earth and believe in the name of the Lord of Spirits forever."

**44** Also another phenomenon I saw in regard to the lightnings, how some of the stars arise and become lightnings and cannot part with their new form[AA].

---

[W] Proverbs 1:20-33

[X] The twelve constellations are about 30° each around the Zodiac.

[Y] Lightening storms come in the spring and fall, marking the beginnings of the two Jewish calendar years.

[Z] Or parable; constellations are pictures of prophecy throughout history.

[AA] Or cannot leave anything behind them.

# Second Parable 45-57

**45** And this is the second parable concerning those who deny the name of the dwelling-place of the holy ones and the Lord of Spirits. ²They will not ascend into the heaven, nor will they come on the earth; such will be the lot of the sinners who deny the name of the Lord of Spirits, who are thus preserved for the day of suffering and tribulation. ³On that day My Elect One [Messiah] will sit on the throne of glory, and will try their works.[A] Their places of rest will be innumerable, and their souls will grow strong when they see My Elect One, and those who have called upon My glorious name.[B] ⁴Then will I cause My Elect One to dwell among them; and I will transform the heaven and make it an eternal blessing and light. ⁵And I will transform the earth and make it a blessing. And I will cause My elect ones to dwell upon it, but the sinners and criminals will not set foot on it. ⁶For I have provided for, and satisfied with peace, My righteous ones, and have caused them to dwell before Me; but for the sinners there is an impending judgment with Me, so that I will destroy them from the face of the earth.

---

[A] For the Father judgeth no man, but hath committed all judgment unto the Son: *John 5:22*

[B] The only way to be saved is by believing on the name of the Messiah. "Neither is there salvation in any other: for there is none other name under heaven given among men, whereby we must be saved." *Acts 4:12*

# 46

There I saw One who was ancient,[C] and His head was white like wool[D], and with Him was another being whose countenance had the appearance of a man, but his face was full of graciousness, like one of the holy angels. [2]And I asked the angel who went with me and showed me all the secret things, concerning this Son of Man[E] [Messiah], who He was, and where He was from, and why was He with the Ancient of Days?

[3]He answered and said unto me, "this is the Son of Man who has righteousness, and righteousness dwells in Him, and who reveals all the secret treasures, because the Lord of Spirits has chosen Him, and whose lot has the pre-eminence before the Lord of Spirits in uprightness forever. [4]And this Son of Man whom you have seen will raise up the kings and the mighty from their seats, and the strong from their thrones, and will loosen the reins of the strong, and break the teeth of the sinners. [5]He will expel the kings from their thrones and kingdoms, because they do not exalt and praise Him, nor humbly acknowledge that their kingdoms were given to them. [6]And He will expel the countenance of the strong, and shame will fill them. Darkness will be their dwelling, and worms will be their bed, and they will have no hope of rising from their beds, because they do not exalt the name of the Lord of

---

[C] Literally "head of days"

[D] ...the Ancient of Days did sit, whose garment was white as snow, and the hair of his head like the pure wool: his throne was like the fiery flame, and his wheels as burning fire. *Daniel 7:9*

[E] I saw in the night visions, and, behold, one like the Son of man came with the clouds of heaven, and came to the Ancient of Days, and they brought Him near before Him. *Daniel 7:13*

Spirits. [7]And these are they who judge the stars of heaven, and raise their hands against the Most High, and tread upon the earth and dwell upon it. All their deeds are evil; their power is in their riches, and their faith is in the gods which they have made with their hands. They deny the name of the Lord of Spirits; [8]they will be cast out of the houses of His congregations, and from the faithful who hang upon the name of the Lord of Spirits."

# 47 Bema Judgment Seat

In those days the prayers of the righteous and the blood of the Righteous One will ascend from the earth before the Lord of Spirits. [2]In those days the holy ones who dwell above in the heavens will unite with one voice to supplicate, pray, praise, give thanks, and bless the name of the Lord of Spirits on behalf of the blood of the Righteous One which has been shed;[F] and, that the prayer of the righteous may not be in vain before the Lord of Spirits, that judgment may be done unto them, and that they may not have to suffer forever.

[3]In those days, I saw the Ancient of Days seated upon His throne of glory, and the books[G] of the living were opened before Him, and all His host which is in heaven above stood before Him. [4]The hearts of the holy ones were filled with joy, because the number of the righteous was

---

[F] Messiah's shed blood was necessary for salvation.

[G] For we must all appear before the judgment seat of Christ; that every one may receive the things done in his body, according to that he hath done, whether it be good or bad. *2 Corinthians 5:10*

fulfilled[H], and the prayer of the righteous had been heard, and the blood of the Righteous One had been required before the Lord of Spirits.

**48** At that place I saw the inexhaustible fountain of righteousness, and around it were many fountains of wisdom, and all the thirsty drank of them, and were filled with wisdom, and their dwellings were with the righteous, holy, and elect. [2]At that hour the Son of Man[I] was called into the presence of the Lord of Spirits, and named before the Ancient of Days. [3]Before the sun and the signs were created, before the stars of the heaven were made[J], His name was named before the Lord of Spirits. [4]He will be a staff[K] to the righteous whereon to stay themselves and not fall; and he will be the light of the nations[L], and the hope of those who are sick of heart. [5]All who dwell on earth will fall down and bend the knee[M] before Him, and will praise, bless, and sing psalms before

---

[H] A specific number of years God allotted for human history: 7,000 years according to chapter 93.

[I] Jesus existed before anything was created, John 1:1;

[J] God, who at sundry times and in divers manners spake in time past unto the fathers by the prophets, hath in these last days spoken unto us by his Son, whom he hath appointed heir of all things, by whom also he made the worlds; *Hebrews 1:1-2*

[K] A bruised reed shall he not break, and smoking flax shall he not quench, till he send forth judgment unto victory. *Matthew 12:20; Isaiah 42:3*

[L] That Christ should suffer, and that He should be the first that should rise from the dead, and should shew light unto the people, and to the Gentiles. *Acts 26:23*

[M] That at the name of Jesus every knee should bow, of things in heaven, and things in earth, and things under the earth; And that every tongue should confess that Jesus Christ is Lord, to the glory of God the Father. *Philippians 2:10-11* and *Isaiah 45:23*

the Lord of Spirits. [6]For this reason He was chosen and hidden before Him, before the creation of the world and will be with Him throughout all eternity.[N] [7]And the wisdom of the Lord of Spirits has revealed Him to the holy and righteous; for He has preserved the lot of the righteous[O], because they have hated and despised this world of unrighteousness, and have hated all its works and ways in the name of the Lord of Spirits. For in His name they are saved[P], and He will be the avenger of their lives. [8]In these days the kings of the earth will be downcast in countenance, and the strong who possess the land will be bent down because of the works of their hands, for on the day of their terror, the day of tribulation, their souls will not be saved. [9]I will give them over into the hands of My Elect One as straw in the fire; so will they burn before the face of the Holy One. As lead in the water will they sink before the face of the righteous so that no trace of them will ever be found. [10]On the day of their trouble there will be rest on the earth, and before Him they will fall and not rise again. And there will be no one to take them with their hands and raise them up, for they have denied the Lord of Spirits and His Messiah. The name of the Lord of Spirits be blessed.

---

[N] The Son of Man exists with God the Father throughout all eternity.

[O] While I was with them in the world, I kept them in thy name: those that thou gavest me I have kept, and none of them is lost. *John 17:12*

[P] Neither is there salvation in any other: for there is none other name under heaven given among men, whereby we must be saved. *Acts 4:12.*

# 49

For wisdom is poured out like water, and glory does not cease before Him forever. [2]For He is mighty in all the secrets of righteousness, and unrighteousness will disappear as a shadow, and have no continuance; because the Elect One has arisen before the Lord of Spirits, and His glory is forever, and His might unto all generations. [3]In Him dwells the spirit of wisdom, the spirit of insight, the spirit of understanding and of might, and the spirits of those who have fallen asleep in righteousness. [4]He will judge the secret things, and none will be able to utter a lying word before Him; for He is the Elect One before the Lord of Spirits according to His good pleasure.

# 50

In those days a change[Q] will take place for the holy and elect, and the light of days will abide upon them, and glory and honour will turn to the holy. [2]On the day of tribulation on which evil will gather against the sinners, the righteous will overcome in the name of the Lord of Spirits. He will cause the others to witness it that they may repent and cease the works of their hands. [3]They will have no honour before the Lord of Spirits, yet through His name will they be saved.[R] And the Lord of Spirits will have mercy on them, for His mercy is great. [4]He is righteous also in His judgment. Unrighteousness will not be able to stand in the presence

---

[Q] The Rapture will occur in order to lead the others to repentance. "Behold, I shew you a mystery; We shall not all sleep, but we shall all be changed, in a moment, in the twinkling of an eye, at the last trump: for the trumpet shall sound, and the dead shall be raised incorruptible, and we shall be changed." *1 Corinthians 15:51-52*

[R] Salvation through repentance and belief in His Name.

of His glory. Whoever will not repent will perish before Him. [5]"From now on I will have no mercy upon them," says the Lord of Spirits.

# 51

In those days will the earth also give back that which has been entrusted to it, and Sheol also will give back that which it has received, and hell will give back that which it owes.[S] [2]And He will choose the righteous and holy from among them, for the day has come that they should be saved. [3]In those days the Elect One will sit on His throne;[T] and His mouth will teach all the secrets of wisdom and counsel, for the Lord of Spirits has given them to Him and has glorified Him. [4]In those days will the mountains leap like rams, and the hills also will skip like lambs satisfied with milk, and the faces of all the angels in heaven will be lit up with joy. [5]For in those days the Elect One will arise[U], and the earth will rejoice, and the righteous will dwell upon it, and the elect will walk on it.

# 52 The Mountains

After those days in that place where I had seen all the visions of the secrets — for I had been carried off in a whirlwind and they had borne me toward the west —

---

[S] "...death and hell delivered up the dead which were in them: and they were judged every man according to their works." *Revelation 20:13*

[T] "He shall be great, and shall be called the Son of the Highest: and the Lord God shall give unto him the throne of his father David: And he shall reign over the house of Jacob for ever; and of his kingdom there shall be no end." *Luke 1:32-33*

[U] Messiah will resurrect from the dead.

[2]there my eyes saw all the secret things of heaven that will be on earth: a mountain of iron, and a mountain of copper, and a mountain of silver, and a mountain of gold, and a mountain of soft metal, and a mountain of lead. [3]And I asked the angel who went with me, saying, "What are these things which I have seen in secret?"

[4]And he said unto me, "All these things which you have seen will serve the dominion of His Messiah, that He may be powerful on the earth." [5]And that angel of peace answered, saying unto me, "Wait a little, and there will be revealed unto you all the secret things which surround the Lord of Spirits. [6]These mountains which thine eyes have seen: the mountain of iron, and the mountain of copper, and the mountain of silver, and the mountain of gold, and the mountain of soft metal, and the mountain of lead, all these will melt as wax before fire in the presence of the Elect One. And like the water which comes down from above on these mountains, they will become powerless before His feet. [7]And it will come to pass in those days that none will be able to save themselves with gold or silver, or flee. [8]There will be no iron for war, no material for a breastplate, copper will be of no service, and soft metal will not be esteemed, and lead will not be desired. [9]And all these things will disappear and be destroyed from the face of the earth, when the Elect One will appear before the face of the Lord of Spirits."

53 There I saw a deep valley with open mouths; and all who dwell on the earth, sea, and islands will bring gifts and presents and tokens of homage to Him, but

that deep valley will not become full. [2]The sinners commit lawless deeds with their hands, and devour all whom they lawlessly oppress, but they will be destroyed before the face of the Lord of Spirits, and they will be banished from off the face of His earth forever. [3]For I saw all the angels of punishment abiding there and preparing all the instruments of Satan. [4]And I asked the angel of peace who went with me, "For whom are they preparing these instruments?"

[5]And he said unto me, "They prepare these instruments to destroy the kings and the mighty of this earth. [6]And after this the Righteous and Elect One will cause the house of His congregation to appear. From then on, they will be no more hindered in the name of the Lord of Spirits. [7]These mountains of the earth will not stand against His righteousness; but they will be as a fountain of water, and the righteous will have rest from the oppression of sinners."

## 54 Azazel Imprisoned in lowest Hell
And I looked and turned to another part of the earth and saw there a deep valley with burning fire. [2]And they brought the kings and the mighty and began to cast them into this deep valley. [3]There I saw how they made their instruments, iron chains of immeasurable weight. [4]I asked the angel of peace who went with me, saying: "For whom are these chains being prepared?" [5]And he said unto me, "These are being prepared for the hosts of Azazel, so that they may imprison them and cast them

into the lowest abyss[V], and they will cover their jaws with rough stones as the Lord of Spirits commanded. [6]Michael, Gabriel, Raphael, and Phanuel will take hold of them on that great day, and cast them on that day into the burning furnace, that the Lord of Spirits may take vengeance on them for their unrighteousness in becoming subject to Satan[W] and leading astray those who dwell on the earth."

*[7]In those days will punishment come from the Lord of Spirits, and He will open all the chambers of waters which are above the heavens, and of the fountains which are beneath the earth. [8]And all the waters will be joined with the waters: that which is above the heavens is the masculine, and the water which is beneath the earth is the feminine. [9]And they will destroy all who dwell on the earth and those who dwell under the ends of the heaven. [10]Through this they will know their unrighteousness which they have done on the earth. Then by these will they perish.*

## 55 The Rainbow

*After that the Ancient of Days repented and said, "In vain have I destroyed all who dwell on the earth." [2]And He swore by His great name, "I will never do this again to those who dwell on the earth, and I will set a sign in the heaven. And this will be a*

---

[V] The bottomless pit of Revelation 20:3 and Tartarus of 2 Peter 2:4.
[W] Azazel and his angels became subject to Satan

*pledge of fidelity between Me and them forever, so long as heaven is above the earth.*[X]

[3]"And this is in accordance with My command, when I desire to take hold of them by the hand of the angels on the day of tribulation and pain. Until this, My anger and My wrath abide upon them," says God, the Lord of Spirits. [4]You mighty kings who dwell on the earth, you will behold My Elect One, how He sits on the throne of glory and judges Azazel, and all his associates, and all his hosts in the name of the Lord of Spirits."

## 56 Fallen Angels Imprisoned

I saw there the hosts of the angels of punishment going, and they held chains of iron and bronze.[Y] [2]And I asked the angel of peace who went with me, saying, "To whom are these who hold the chains going?"

[3]And he said unto me, "To their chosen and beloved ones, that they may be cast into the chasm of the abyss of the valley. [4]Then that valley will be filled with their chosen and beloved, and the days of their lives will be at an end, and the days of their error, from that time on, will not be reckoned.

### Iran invades Israel

[5]"And in those days the angels will return and come to the kings of the east along with the Medes and Persians

---

[X] Enoch 54:7 through 55:2 seems to be a Gnostic insert and completely out of place in the text.

[Y] Iron and bronze symbolize complete protection or incarceration. See Deuteronomy 33:25

[Iran]. They will stir up these kings, so that a spirit of unrest will come over them, and they will rouse them from their thrones, that they may break forth as lions from their lairs, and as hungry wolves among their flocks. <sup>6</sup>They will go up and tread underfoot the land of His elect ones [Israel] and the land of His elect ones will be before them a threshing-floor [Temple Mount] and a highway. <sup>7</sup>But the city of my righteous [Jerusalem] will be a hindrance to their horses, and they will begin to fight among themselves. And their right hand will be strong against themselves, and a man will not know his brother, nor a son his father or his mother, till there be no number of their corpses through their own slaughter<sup>Z</sup>, — their punishment will not be in vain. <sup>8</sup>In those days the mouth of Sheol will open, and they will be swallowed up in it. Sheol will devour and destroy the sinners in the presence of the elect."

# 57 Gog-Magog War <sup>AA</sup>

It came to pass after this that I saw another host of men riding on wagons [tanks], and coming on the winds [planes and missiles] from the east, and from the west *to* the south.<sup>BB</sup> <sup>2</sup>The noise of their wagons was heard, and when this turmoil took place, the holy ones from heaven

---

<sup>Z</sup> And I will call for a sword against him throughout all my mountains, saith the Lord GOD: every man's sword shall be against his brother. *Ezekiel 38:21*

<sup>AA</sup> Ezekiel 38-39; Enoch may be one of the prophets referred to in Ezekiel 38:17

<sup>BB</sup> Zechariah's horsemen? East and west to the south? Armageddon kings of east and west ~ Russia and China? Or Gog Magog - "Thus saith the Lord GOD; Art thou he of whom I have spoken in old time by My servants the prophets ...?" *Ezekiel 38:17*

noticed it, and the pillars of the earth were moved from their place [nuclear], and their sound was heard from the one end of heaven to the other, in ONE day. [3]And they will all fall down and bend the knee[CC] to the Lord of Spirits.

This is the end of the second parable.

---

[CC] That at the name of Jesus every knee should bow, of things in heaven, and things in earth, and things under the earth; and that every tongue should confess that Jesus Christ is Lord, to the glory of God the Father. *Philippians 2:10-11* and *Isaiah 45:23*

# Third Parable 58-71

**58** And I began to speak the third parable concerning the righteous and elect. "²Blessed are you righteous and elect, for glorious will be your lot. ³And the righteous will be in the light of the sun and the elect in the light of eternal life. The days of their life will be unending, and the days of the holy without number. ⁴And they will seek the light and find righteousness with the Lord of Spirits. There will be peace to the righteous in the name of the eternal Lord.

⁵After this it will be said to the holy in heaven that they should seek out the secrets of righteousness, the heritage of faith, for it has become bright as the sun upon earth, and the darkness is past. ⁶And there will be a light that never ends, and no limit of days, for the darkness will be destroyed first, and the light established before the Lord of Spirits, and the light of uprightness will be established forever before the Lord of Spirits."

**59** In those days my eyes saw the secrets of the lightnings, and of the lights, and their judgments; and they flashed for a blessing or a curse as the Lord of Spirits desired. ²And there I saw the secrets of the thunder, and how when it resounds above in the heaven, its sound is heard, and he showed me the judgments executed on the earth, whether they be for a blessing or a curse, according to the word of the Lord of Spirits. ³And after that all the secrets of the stars and lightnings were shown to me, and they shine for blessing and for satisfaction.

**60** *A Fragment of the Book of Noah[A]*
*In the year five hundred, in the seventh month, on the fourteenth day of the month in the life of Enoch:[B] in that parable I saw how the heaven of heavens shook tremendously[C], and the host of the Most High, and the angels, a thousand thousands and ten thousand times ten thousand, were greatly disturbed. [2]And the Ancient of Days sat on His glorious throne and the angels and the righteous stood around Him. [3]Great fear and trembling seized me, and my loins gave way, and my whole body collapsed, and I fell upon my face. [4]Michael sent another angel from among the holy ones and he raised me up. As he raised me up, my spirit returned; for I had not been able to endure the sight of this host and the commotion and the quaking of the heaven. [5]Michael said unto me, "Why do you tremble so at this vision? Until this day lasted the day of His mercy; and He has been merciful and long-suffering[D] towards those who dwell on the earth. [6]When the day, and the power, punishment,*

---

[A] Chapter 60 is most likely another Gnostic insertion; it should be disregarded.

[B] Or Noah; Enoch was raptured at the age of 365.

[C] Whose voice then shook the earth: but now he hath promised, saying, Yet once more I shake not the earth only, but also heaven. *Hebrews 12:26-29*

[D] The Lord is not slack concerning his promise, as some men count slackness; but is longsuffering to us-ward, not willing that any should perish, but that all should come to repentance. *2 Peter 3:9*

*and judgment comes, which the Lord of Spirits has prepared for those who do not bow to the righteous law, and for those who deny the righteous judgment, and for those who take His name in vain — that day a covenant is prepared for the elect, but an inquisition for sinners. ⁷And on that day were two monsters parted, a female monster named Leviathan^E to dwell in the abysses of the ocean over the fountains of the waters. ⁸But the male is named Behemoth, who occupied with his breast a waste wilderness named Duidain, [Dendain: the judgment of the judge] on the east of the garden where the elect and righteous dwell, where my grandfather was taken up. He was the seventh from Adam, who was the first man whom the Lord of Spirits created. ⁹And I asked the other angel to show me the might of those monsters, how they were separated on one day, and the one cast into the abyss of the sea, and the other unto the dry land of the wilderness. ¹⁰And he said to me: "son of man, what you desire to know is a secret."*

*¹¹The other angel, who went with me and showed me what was secret, told me what is first and last from beneath the depth of the earth to the height of heaven, and from the foundation to the ends of the heaven. ¹²And [he showed me] the chambers of the winds, and how the winds are divided, and weighed, and how the portals of the winds are reckoned, each*

---

^E Thou brakest the heads of leviathan in pieces, and gavest him to be meat to the people inhabiting the wilderness. *Psalms 74:14*

*according to the power of the wind. And [he showed me] the power of the lights of the moon, and according to the power that is fitting, and the divisions of the stars according to their names[F], and how all the divisions are divided. [13]And [he showed me] the thunders according to the places where they fall, and all the divisions that are made among the flashes of lightning, and their host that they may at once obey. [14]For the thunder has places of rest while it is waiting for its peal; and the thunder and lightning are inseparable, and although not one, they both go together through the wind and are not separated. [15]For when the lightning flashes, the thunder makes its sound, and the wind causes a rest during the peal, and divides equally between them; for the treasury of their peals is like the sand, and each one of them as it peals is held in with a bridle, and turned back by the power of the spirit, and pushes forward according to the many directions of the earth. [16]And the wind of the sea is strong like a man, and by its strength it draws the waves back with a rein, and in like manner it is driven forward and disperses amid all the shores of the earth.*

*[17]And the spirit of the hoar-frost is its own angel, and the spirit of the hail is a good angel. [18]And the spirit of the snow has forsaken his chambers on account of his strength, and it has a special spirit, and that which ascends from it is like smoke, and its name is frost. [19]And the spirit of the mist is not*

---

[F] See chapter 43:1

united with them in their chambers, but it has a special chamber; for its course is glorious both in light and in darkness, and in winter and in summer, and in its chamber is an angel. [20]And the spirit of the dew has its dwelling at the ends of the heaven, and is connected with the chambers of the rain, and its course is in winter and summer: and its clouds and the clouds of the mist are connected, and the one gives to the other. [21]And when the spirit of the rain goes forth from its chamber, the angels come and open the chamber and lead it out, and when it is diffused over the whole earth it unites with the water on the earth. [22]For the waters are for those who dwell on the earth; for they are nourishment for the earth from the Most High who is in heaven: therefore there is a measure for the rain, and the angels take charge of it. [23]All these things I saw towards the Garden of the Righteous.

[24]And the angel of peace who was with me said to me, "These two monsters will feed; according to the greatness of God, these two will slay the children with their mothers and the children with their fathers. [25]When the punishment from the Lord of Spirits will rest upon them, it will rest in order that the punishment of the Lord of Spirits may not come in vain. Afterwards the judgment will take place according to His mercy and His patience[G]."

---

[G] Or despisest thou the riches of his goodness and forbearance and longsuffering; not knowing that the goodness of God leadeth thee to repentance? *Romans 2:4*

# 61

And I saw in those days how long cords were given to those angels, and they took to themselves wings and flew, and they went toward the north. ²And I asked the angel, saying, "Why did they fly off with these cords?"

And he said unto me, "They have gone to measure." ³And the angel who went with me said unto me, "These will bring the measuring ropes of the righteous, so that they may support themselves on the name of the Lord of Spirits forever. ⁴The elect will begin to dwell with the elect[H], and those are the measures which will be given to faith, and will strengthen the word of righteousness. ⁵And these measures will reveal all the secrets of the depths of the earth, and those who have been destroyed by the desert, and those who have been devoured by the beasts, and the fish of the sea, that they may return and support themselves on the day of the Elect One; for none will be destroyed before the Lord of Spirits, and none can be destroyed.[I]

⁶All who dwell above in the heaven received a command and one power, one voice, and one light fire was given them. ⁷That One first they blessed, exalted, glorified with

---

[H] For the Lord himself shall descend from heaven with a shout, with the voice of the archangel, and with the trump of God: and the dead in Christ shall rise first: then we which are alive and remain shall be caught up together with them in the clouds, to meet the Lord in the air: and so shall we ever be with the Lord. *1 Thessalonians 4:16-17*

[I] And *though* after my skin *worms* destroy this *body*, yet in my flesh shall I see God: *Job 19:26*

wisdom, and showed that they were wise in speech and in the spirit of life.

[8]The Lord of Spirits placed the Elect One on His glorious throne, and He will judge all the works of the holy in heaven, and their deeds will be weighed on scales. [9]When He will lift up His countenance to judge their secret ways according to the word of the name of the Lord of Spirits, and their path according to the way of the righteous judgment of the Lord of Spirits, then will they all speak with one voice and bless, exalt, and glorify the name of the Lord of Spirits.

[10]And He will summon all the host of the heavens, and all the holy ones above, and the host of God: the cherubim, seraphim, and ophannim, and all the angels of power, and all the angels of principalities, and the Elect One, and the other powers on the earth and over the water. [11]On that day, they will raise one voice, and bless, glorify, and exalt in the spirit of faith, wisdom, patience, mercy, judgment, peace, and in the spirit of goodness, and will all say with one voice, "Blessed is He, and may the name of the Lord of Spirits be blessed forever." [12]All who do not sleep in the high heavens will bless Him; all the holy ones who are in heaven will bless Him, and all the elect who dwell in the garden of life, and every spirit of light who is able to bless, and glorify, and exalt Your name forever and ever. [13]For great is the mercy of the Lord of Spirits, and He is slow to anger, and all His works and all that He has created He has revealed to the righteous and elect in the name of the Lord of Spirits.

# 62 Second Coming

Thus the Lord commanded the kings, mighty, exalted, and those who dwell on the earth, and said, "Open your eyes and lift up your horns if you are able to recognize the Elect One.[J]" [2]And the Lord of Spirits seated Him on the throne of His glory, and the spirit of righteousness was poured out upon Him, and the word of His mouth[K] slew all the sinners, and the unrighteous were destroyed from before His face. [3]There will stand up in that day all the kings, the mighty, the exalted, and those who hold the earth, and they will see and recognize how He sits on His glorious throne, and righteousness is judged before Him, and no lying word is spoken before Him.

[4]Then will pain come upon them as on a woman in travail, in a hard birth, when her child enters the mouth of the womb, and she has pain in giving birth. [5]And one portion of them will look on the other, and they will be terrified. They will be downcast of countenance and pain will seize them when they see that Son of Man[L] sitting on the throne of His glory.

---

[J] Enoch implies some will recognize the Messiah when He returns.

[K] And then shall that Wicked be revealed, whom the Lord shall consume with the spirit of His mouth, and shall destroy with the brightness of His coming: *2 Thessalonians 2:8;*
And out of his mouth goeth a sharp sword, that with it he should smite the nations: *Revelation 19:15*

[L] Some manuscripts have "Son of Woman" implying a virgin birth; Isaiah 7:14

<sup>6</sup>And the kings and the mighty and all who possess the earth will bless and glorify and exalt Him who rules over all, who was hidden. <sup>7</sup>For from the beginning the Son of Man was hidden, and the Most High preserved Him in the presence of His might, and revealed Him to the elect. <sup>8</sup>And the congregation of the elect and holy will be sown and all the elect will stand before Him on that day. <sup>9</sup>And all the kings and the mighty and the exalted and those who rule the earth will fall down before Him on their faces, and worship and set their hope upon that Son of Man, and petition Him and ask Him for mercy. <sup>10</sup>Nevertheless, that Lord of Spirits will so press them that they will hastily go forth from His presence, and their faces will be filled with shame and the darkness grow deeper on their faces. <sup>11</sup>He will deliver them to the angels for punishment, to execute vengeance on them because they have oppressed His children and His elect. <sup>12</sup>They will be a spectacle for the righteous and for His elect. They will rejoice over them, because the wrath of the Lord of Spirits rests upon them, and His sword is drunk with their blood.

<sup>13</sup>The righteous and elect will be saved on that day, and they will never again see the face of the sinners and unrighteous. <sup>14</sup>The Lord of Spirits will abide with them, and with the Son of Man will they eat, lie down, and rise up with Him forever. <sup>15</sup>The righteous and elect will rise from the earth, and cease to be of downcast countenance, and they will be clothed with garments of eternal life. <sup>16</sup>These will be the garments of life from the Lord of

Spirits, and your garments will not grow old, nor your glory pass away before the Lord of Spirits.

**63** In those days will the mighty kings who possess the earth implore Him to grant them a little respite from His angels of punishment to whom they were delivered, that they might fall down and worship before the Lord of Spirits, and confess their sins before Him. ²And they will bless and glorify the Lord of Spirits, and say, "Blessed is the Lord of Spirits and the Lord of kings, and the Lord of the mighty and the Lord of the rulers, and the Lord of glory and the Lord of wisdom, and every secret is clear: ³Your power from generation to generation, and Your glory forever. Deep are all Your innumerable secrets, and Your righteousness is beyond reckoning. ⁴Now we know that we should glorify and bless the Lord of kings, who rules over all kings."

⁵They will say, "Who will give us rest to glorify, give thanks, and confess our faith before His glory? ⁶Now we long for a little rest but cannot find it. We are driven away and cannot obtain it, and light has vanished before us, and darkness is our dwelling-place forever. ⁷For we have not believed before Him nor glorified the name of the Lord of Spirits, but our hope was in the sceptre of our kingdom and glory. ⁸And in the day of our suffering and tribulation He did not save us; and we find no respite for confession that our Lord is true in all His works, judgments, and

justice and His judgments have no respect of persons.[M]
[9]We will disappear before His face on account of our works, and all our sins are reckoned up in righteousness."

[10]Now they will say unto themselves, "Our souls are full of unrighteous gain, but it does not prevent us from going into the painful flames of hell." [11]After that their faces will be filled with darkness and shame before that Son of Man, and they will be driven from His presence, and the sword will abide before His face in their midst.

[12]Thus said the Lord of Spirits, "This is the ordinance and judgment with respect to the mighty and the kings and the exalted and those who possess the earth before the Lord of Spirits."

**64** And I saw other forms hidden in that place. [2]I heard the voice of the angel saying, "These are the angels who descended from heaven to earth, and revealed what was hidden to the children of men, and seduced the children of men into committing sin."

**65** *Another Gnostic Insert*
*In those days Noah saw the earth that it had sunk down[N] and its destruction was imminent. [2]He arose from there and went to the ends of the earth, and called to his grandfather Enoch. And Noah said*

---

[M] But he that doeth wrong shall receive for the wrong which he hath done: and there is no respect of persons. *Colossians 3:25*; see also James 2:1,9 and 1 Peter 1:17

[N] Inclined or tilted

three times with an embittered voice, "Hear me, hear me, hear me." ³He said unto him, "Tell me what it is that is going on in the earth that the earth is in such evil plight and shaken? I do not wish to perish with it."

⁴And thereupon there was a great quaking on the earth, and a voice was heard from heaven, and I fell on my face. ⁵Enoch, my grandfather, came and stood by me, and said unto me, "Why have you bitterly cried unto me? ⁶A command has gone forth from the presence of the Lord concerning those who dwell on the earth, that their end is at hand, because they know all the secrets of the angels, and all the violence of the adversaries^O, and all their powers — the power of secrets of sorcery and the making of molten images for the whole earth; ⁷how silver is produced from the dust of the earth, and how soft metal originates in the earth. ⁸For lead and tin are not produced from the earth like the first, they are produced as by-products of the fountain, and an angel stands therein, and that angel is excellent."

⁹And after that my grandfather Enoch took hold of me by my hand and raised me up, and said unto me, "Go, for I have asked the Lord of Spirits as touching this quaking on the earth." ¹⁰He said unto me, "Because of their unrighteousness their

---

^O Literally "Satans"

*judgment has been determined; I will not recount the months for them, which they have inquired as to when the earth and those who dwell upon it will be destroyed. <sup>11</sup>They have no place of repentance forever, because they have shown them what was hidden, and they are the damned. But as for you, my son, the Lord of Spirits knows that you are pure and guiltless of this reproach concerning the secrets. <sup>12</sup>He has destined thy name to be among the holy, and will preserve you among those who dwell on the earth, and has destined your righteous seed both for kingship and for great honors, and from thy seed<sup>P</sup> will proceed a fountain of the righteous and holy without number forever."*

**66** *After that he showed me the angels of punishment who are prepared to come and let loose all the mighty waters which are beneath in the earth in order to bring judgment and destruction on all who dwell on the earth. <sup>2</sup>And the Lord of Spirits commanded to the angels who were going forth, that they should not cause the waters to rise, but should hold them in check; for those angels were over the mighty waters. <sup>3</sup>And I went away from the presence of Enoch.*

**67** *And in those days the word of God came unto me, and He said unto me, "Noah, thy*

---

<sup>P</sup> The Messiah comes though his descendants.

*lot has come up before Me, a lot blameless, with love and uprightness. [2]And now the angels[Q] are making a wooden building, and when they have completed that task, I will place My hand upon it and preserve it. And there will come forth from it the seed of life, and a change will set in so that the earth will not remain without inhabitant. [3]I will hold fast thy seed before Me forever, and I will spread abroad those who dwell with you. It will not be unfruitful on the face of the earth, but it will be blessed and multiply on the earth in the name of the Lord."*

*[4]He will imprison those angels who have shown unrighteousness, in that burning valley[R] which my grandfather Enoch had formerly shown to me in the west among the mountains of gold, silver, iron, and soft metal, and tin. [5]I saw that valley in which there was a great quaking and a convulsion of the waters. [6]When all this took place, the quake produced fiery molten metal from which was produced a smell of sulphur, and it poured into those waters, and that valley of the angels who had led astray (mankind) burned beneath that earth. [7]Through that valley proceed rivers of fire, where these angels who had led astray those who dwell upon the earth are condemned. [8]In those days, those waters will serve for the kings, the mighty, the exalted, and those who dwell on the earth, for the healing of the body, but*

---

[Q] Genesis records Noah and his sons made the Ark, not angels
[R] Unknown Valley

*for the punishment of the spirit; because their spirit is full of lust, that they may be punished in their bodies. For they have denied the Lord of Spirits and see their punishment daily, and yet believe not in His name. [9]In proportion as the burning of their bodies becomes severe, a corresponding change will take place in their spirit forever; for no one will utter an idle word before the Lord of Spirits. [10]For the judgment will come upon them, because they believe in the lust of their flesh and deny the Spirit of the Lord. [11]Those same waters will undergo a change in those days; for when those angels are punished in these waters, these water-springs will change their temperature, and when the angels ascend, this water of the springs will change and become cold. [12]And I heard Michael answering and saying, "This judgment wherewith the angels are judged is a testimony for the kings and the mighty who possess the earth. [13]Because these waters of judgment are to heal the earth by destroying their bodies, therefore they will not see and will not believe that those waters will change and become a fire which burns forever."*

*68 After that, my grandfather Enoch gave me the teaching of all the secrets in the book, and the parables which had been given to him, and he put them together for me in the words of the book of the parables.*

[2]On that day Michael answered Raphael and said, "The power of the Spirit makes me tremble because of the severity of the judgment of the secrets, the judgment of the angels. Who can endure the severe judgment which has been executed, and before which they melt away?" [3]Michael continued, and said to Raphael, "Who is he whose heart is not softened concerning it, and whose reins are not troubled by this word of judgment that has come upon them because of those who have thus led them out?" [4]And it came to pass when he stood before the Lord of Spirits, Michael said thus to Raphael, "I will not watch over them as the eye of the Lord; for the Lord of Spirits has been angry with them because they do as if they were gods. [5]Therefore, all that is hidden will come upon them forever; for neither angel nor man will have his portion in it, but alone they have received their judgment forever.[S]"

# 69 The Chiefs of the Angels

After this judgment, they will terrify and make them to tremble because they have shown this to those who dwell on the earth. [2] And behold the names of those angels; and these are their names: the first of them is Semyaza, the second Artaqifa, and the third Armen, the fourth Kokabel, the fifth Turael, the sixth Rumial, the seventh Danial, the eighth Neqael, the ninth Baraqel, the tenth Azazel, the eleventh Armaros, the twelfth Batarial,

---

[S] After the judgment of the two hundred, no angel will dare crossbread with humans because the punishment is so severe. Men will tamper with genetics in the last days, but there will be no more angelic re-creations or Nephilim.

the thirteenth Busaseial, the fourteenth Hananel, the fifteenth Turel, and the sixteenth Simapesiel, the seventeenth Jetrel, the eighteenth Tumael, the nineteenth Turel, the twentieth Rumael, the twenty-first Azazel.[T]
[3]These are the chiefs of their angels and their names, and their chiefs over hundreds and over fifties and over tens.

## The Teaching of the Angels
[4]The name of the first is Jeqon. He is the one who led astray all the sons of God, and brought them down to the earth, and led them astray through the daughters of men.

[5]The second was named Asbeel. He imparted to the holy sons of God evil counsel, and led them astray so that they defiled their bodies with the daughters of men.

## Weapons
[6]The third was named Gadreel. He it is who showed the children of men all the blows of death. And he led astray Eve, and showed the weapons of death to the sons of men: the shield, the coat of mail, and the sword for battle, and all the weapons of death to the children of men. [7]From his hand they have proceeded against those who dwell on the earth from that day and forever.

## Legal Manipulation
[8]The fourth was named Penemue. He taught the children of men the bitter and the sweet, and he taught them all the secrets of their wisdom. [9]And he instructed mankind in

---

[T] Compare these 21 to the 18 in Enoch 6:7

writing with ink and paper, and thereby many sinned for all eternity unto this day. [10]For men were not created for such a purpose, to give confirmation to their good faith with pen and ink.[U] [11]For men were created exactly like the angels, to the intent that they should continue pure and righteous, and death (which destroys everything) could not have touched them, but through this their knowledge they are perishing, and through this power it is consuming me.

## Abortion
[12]And the fifth was named Kasdeia, he who showed the children of men all the wicked smiting of spirits and demons, and the smiting of the embryo in the womb[V], that it may pass away, and the smiting of the soul, the bites of the serpent, and the smiting which befalls through the noontide heat, the son of the serpent named Taba'et.

## The Secret Name
[13]This is the number of the Kasbeel, who showed the chief of the oath to the holy ones when he dwelt high above in glory. [14]One angel, named Biqa, requested Michael to show him the hidden name, so he could enunciate it in the oath, so that those might quake before that name and oath, who revealed all that was in secret to the children of men. [15]This is the power of that oath, for it is powerful and strong, and he placed this oath of Akae[W]

---

[U] Legal documents to get out of covenants and contracts.

[V] The fallen angels taught Abortion. See Ancient Book of Jasher 2.

[W] The fallen angels thought by learning the oath of Akae (secret of creation) they might become powerful enough to repel the flood. It

in the hand of Michael. [16]These are the secrets of this oath which strengthened them, and which suspended heaven before the world was created, and forever. [17]And through it the earth was founded upon the water, and from the secret recesses of the mountains come beautiful waters, from the creation of the world and forever. [18]And through that oath the sea was created. And as its foundation He set for it the sand for the time of rage, and it dare not pass beyond it from the creation of the world and forever. [19]And through that oath are the depths made fast, and abide and do not move from their place for forever. [20]And through that oath the sun and moon complete their course, and do not deviate from their ordinance for forever. [21]And through that oath the stars complete their course, and He calls them by their names, and they answer Him for forever. [22]And in like manner the currents of the water, and of the winds, and of all zephyrs[X], and their currents all unite. [23]And there are preserved the voices of the thunder and the light of the lightnings; and there are preserved the chambers of the hail[Y] and the chambers of the hoarfrost, and the chambers of the mist, and the chambers of the rain and the dew. [24]And all these believe and give thanks before the Lord of Spirits, and glorify Him with all their power, and their food is in every act of

---

could also be that they were trying to get the secret name of the Messiah so when He appears He could be killed. The Messiah's name was secret; and He created everything, but the angels thought it was just a magic name. They thought if they learned the secret they would become powerful.

[X] West wind

[Y] Hast thou entered into the treasures of the snow? or hast thou seen the treasures of the hail, *Job 38:22*

thanksgiving. They thank and glorify and exalt the name of the Lord of Spirits forever. [25]This oath is mighty over them and they are preserved by it, and their paths are preserved, and their course is not destroyed.

[26]And there was great joy amongst them, and they blessed and glorified and exalted because the name of that Son of Man[Z] had been revealed unto them. [27]And He sat on His glorious throne and the sum of judgment was given unto the Son of Man, and He caused the sinners to pass away and be destroyed from off the face of the earth, and those who have led the world astray. [28]They will be bound with chains and imprisoned in the assemblage-place of destruction, and all their works will vanish from the face of the earth. [29]From that time on there will be nothing corruptible; for that Son of Man has appeared, and has seated Himself on His glorious throne, and all evil will pass away before His face, and the word of that Son of Man will go forth and be strong before the Lord of Spirits.

This ends the third parable of Enoch

# 70 Enoch's Rapture
It came to pass after this that his name[AA] during his lifetime was elevated to that Son of Man and to the Lord of Spirits from among those who dwell on the earth.

---

[Z] The name of the Son of Man is the secret name - Yeshua or Jesus

[AA] By faith Enoch was translated that he should not see death; and was not found, because God had translated him: for before his translation he had this testimony, that he pleased God. *Hebrews 11:5*

²And he was caught up on the chariots of the Spirit and his name taken out of their midst.<sup>BB</sup> ³From that day I was no longer in their midst; and he set me between the two winds, between the north and the west, where the angels took the cords to measure for me the place for the elect and righteous. ⁴And there I saw the first fathers and the righteous who from the beginning dwell in that place.

71 It came to pass after this that my spirit was translated and it ascended into the heavens; and I saw the holy sons of God. They were stepping on flames of fire. Their garments were white and their raiment and their faces shone like snow. ²And I saw two streams of fire, and the light of that fire shone like hyacinth, and I fell on my face before the Lord of Spirits.

³Then the archangel Michael took me by my right hand, and lifted me up and led me forth into all the secrets of mercy and justice. ⁴And he showed me all the secrets of the ends of the heaven, and all the chambers of all the stars, and all the luminaries, whence they proceed before the face of the holy ones.

⁵My spirit was moved into the heaven of heavens; and I saw there, as it were, a structure built of crystals, and between those crystals tongues of living fire. ⁶My spirit saw how a fire that surrounded that house, on all four sides were streams of living fire. ⁷And round about it

---

BB The Greek of 1 Thessalonians 2:7 has the restrainer being taken "out of the midst." This is the same phrase used here of Enoch's rapture. He was taken "out of the midst."

were seraphim, cherubim, and ophannim; these are they who sleep not, but guard the throne of His glory. $^8$And I saw angels who could not be counted, a thousand thousands, and ten thousand times ten thousand, encircling that house. And Michael, Raphael, Gabriel, Phanuel, and the holy angels who are above the heavens go in and out of that house. $^9$Michael, Gabriel, Raphael, Phanuel, and many holy angels without number came forth from that house. $^{10}$And with them the Ancient of Days$^{CC}$, His head white and pure as wool, and His raiment indescribable. $^{11}$I fell on my face, and all my flesh melted, and my spirit was transfigured; and I cried with a loud voice, with the spirit of power, and blessed and glorified and exalted. $^{12}$And these blessings which went forth out of my mouth were well pleasing before that Ancient of Days. $^{13}$And the Ancient of Days came with Michael, Gabriel, Raphael, and Phanuel, and with thousands and ten thousands of angels without number.

$^{14}$And an angel came and greeted me with his voice, and said unto me, "This is the Son of Man who is born unto righteousness, and righteousness abides over Him, and the righteousness of the Head of Days will not forsake Him." $^{15}$And he said unto me, "He proclaims peace unto you in the name of the world to come; for from there peace has proceeded since the creation of the world, and so will it be unto you forever. $^{16}$All who will walk in His ways (since

---

$^{CC}$ I beheld till the thrones were cast down, and the Ancient of Days did sit, whose garment was white as snow, and the hair of his head like the pure wool: his throne was like the fiery flame, and his wheels as burning fire. *Daniel 7:9*

righteousness never forsakes Him), with Him will be their dwelling-places, and with Him their heritage, and they will not be separated from Him forever. [17]And so there will be length of days with that Son of Man, and the righteous will have peace and an upright way, in the name of the Lord of Spirits forever."

# The Astronomical Calendar 72-82

## 72 The Zodiac and the Solar Year[A]

The book of the courses of the luminaries of the heaven, the relations of each, according to their classes, dominion, and their seasons, according to their names, places of origin, and their months: which Uriel, the holy angel, who was with me, showed me. He showed me exactly how the astrological laws work in regard to all the years of the world,[B] till the new creation is made which endures for all eternity.

[2]And this is the first law of the luminaries: the luminary, the sun, has its rising in the eastern constellations of the heaven, and its setting in the western constellations of the heaven. [3]And I saw six constellations in which the sun rises, and six constellations in which the sun sets. And the moon rises and sets in these constellations, and the brightest stars and how they connect to the lesser stars: six in the east and six in the west, and all following each other in accurately corresponding order; also many decans[C] to the right and left of these constellations.

[4]First there goes forth the great luminary, named the sun, and his circumference is like the circumference of the

---

[A] The sun, moon, and planets travel though the twelve constellations of the Zodiac. Each zodiac sign has three other minor constellations called decans that go with it. Each star and constellation has a Hebrew name that foretells prophecy. See Matthew 2:1-12
[B] The prophetic seven-thousand-year-plan of God - Enoch 93
[C] Hebrew "windows"

heaven, and he is quite filled with illuminating and heating fire. [5]The chariot on which he ascends, the [solar] wind drives, and the sun goes down from the heaven and returns through the north in order to reach the east, and is so guided that he comes to the appropriate constellation and shines in the face of the heaven. [6]In this way he rises in the first month [Nisan] in the great constellation [Aries], which is the fourth[D] of those six constellations in the east. [7]In that fourth constellation from which the sun rises in the first month are twelve decans, from which proceed a flame when they are opened in their season. [8]When the sun rises in the heaven, he comes out of that fourth constellation thirty mornings in succession[E], and sets accurately in the constellation in the west of the heaven. [9]During this period the day is daily lengthened and the night nightly shortened to the thirtieth morning. [10]On that day the day is two parts longer than the night; the day amounts to exactly ten parts day and eight parts night.[F] [11]Then the sun rises from that fourth constellation, and sets in the fourth and returns to the fifth portal of the east thirty mornings, and rises from it and sets in the fifth constellation. [12]From then on, the day becomes longer by two parts and amounts to eleven parts day, and the seven parts night. [13]Then it returns to the east and enters into the sixth constellation, and rises and sets in the sixth constellation thirty-one mornings on account of its sign. [14]On that day the day becomes longer than the night, and

---

[D] Or eighth
[E] The sun moves through a sign of the Zodiac every month.
[F] The Equinox; The twenty-four-hour day is divided into eighteen ninety-minute periods.

the day becomes double the night, twelve parts day and six parts night. [15]The sun is set up to make the day shorter and the night longer, and the sun returns to the east and enters into the sixth constellation, and rises and sets from it thirty mornings. [16]And when thirty mornings are accomplished, the day decreases by exactly one part, eleven parts day and seven parts night. [17]And the sun goes forth from that sixth constellation in the west, and goes to the east and rises in the fifth constellation for thirty mornings, and sets in the west again in the fifth western constellation. [18]On that day the day decreases by two parts, ten parts day and eight parts night. [19]And the sun rises from that fifth constellation and sets in the fifth constellation of the west, and rises in the fourth constellation for thirty-one mornings on account of its sign, and sets in the west. [20]On that day the day is equal with the night, nine parts day and nine parts night.[G] [21]And the sun rises from that constellation and sets in the west, and returns to the east and rises thirty mornings in the third constellation and sets in the west in the third constellation. [22]On that day the night becomes longer and the day shorter, till the thirtieth morning when it is eight parts day and ten parts night. [23]And the sun rises from that third constellation and sets in the third constellation in the west and returns to the east, and for thirty mornings rises in the second constellation in the east, and in like manner sets in the second constellation in the west of the heaven. [24]That day is seven parts day and eleven parts night. [25]And the sun rises on that day from that second

---

[G] This would be true if the observer was on the tropic of Cancer at the summer solstice.

constellation and sets in the west in the second constellation, and returns to the east into the first constellation for thirty-one mornings, and sets in the first constellation in the west of the heaven. [26]And on that day the night becomes so long that it is double the day: six parts day and twelve parts night. [27]Then the sun has completed its cycle of constellations and repeats the cycle again, and enters that portal thirty mornings and sets also in the west opposite to it. [28]And on that night has the night decreased in length by one part; seven parts day and eleven parts night.[29]Then the sun returns and enters into the second constellation in the east, and returns to his course for thirty mornings, rising and setting. [30]And on that day the night decreases in length, eight parts day and ten parts night. [31]And on that day the sun rises from the second constellation, and sets in the west, and returns to the east, and rises in the third constellation for thirty-one mornings, and sets in the west of the heaven. [32]On that day the night decreases to nine parts day and nine parts night, and the night is equal to the day and the year is exactly three hundred and sixty-four[H] days long. [33]And the length of the day and of the night, and the shortness of the day and of the night — by the course of the sun they change. [34]So the course of the sun causes the day to become longer and the night shorter.

[35]This is the law and the course of the sun, and his return, as often as he returns, is sixty times and rises and sets, the great luminary which is called the sun, forever. [36]That

---

[H] Pre-Flood year might have been 364 days long.

which rises is the great luminary, and is so named according to its appearance, according as the Lord commanded. [37]Thus he rises, and sets, and is not decreased, and does not rest, but runs day and night, and his light is sevenfold stronger[I] than that of the moon; but as regards size, they are both equal.[J]

# 73 Lunar Month

After this law I saw another law dealing with the smaller luminary, which is called the moon. [2]And her circumference is like the circumference of the heaven, and her chariot in which she rides is driven by the [solar?] wind, and a measure of light is given to her. [3]Every month her rising and setting changes, and her days are like the days of the sun. And when her light is uniform [full] it amounts to the seventh part of the light of the sun. And thus she rises. [4]Her first phase[K] in the east comes forth on the thirtieth morning; and on that day she becomes visible, and constitutes for you the first phase of the moon on the thirtieth day together with the sun in the portal where the sun rises. [5]The one half of her goes forth by a seventh part, and her whole circumference is empty, without light, with the exception of one-seventh part of the fourteenth parts of light. [6]When she receives one-seventh part of the half of her light, her light amounts to one-seventh part and the half thereof, she sets with the sun. [7]When the sun rises and the moon rises with him and

---

[I] Either the moon used to be much brighter, or by "strength" means the cosmic rays that tan or cause cancer.

[J] The sun and moon look the same size from earth when viewed from earth in spite of the fact that the sun is brighter.

[K] First new moon after the spring equinox.

receives the half of one part of light, and in that night in the beginning of her morning [new moon] the moon sets with the sun, and is invisible that night with the fourteen parts and the half of one of them. [8]And she rises on that day with exactly a seventh part, and comes forth and recedes from the rising of the sun, and in her remaining days she becomes bright in the remaining thirteen parts.

# 74 Lunar Year

I saw another course, a law for her, how according to that law she performs her monthly revolution. [2]And all these Uriel, the holy angel who is the leader of them all, showed me all things; and I wrote down all their positions as he showed them to me. And I wrote down their months as they were, and the appearance of their lights till fifteen days were completed. [3]In seven single parts she completes all her light in the east, and in seven single parts completes all her darkness in the west. [4]In certain months she alters her settings, and in certain months she pursues her own peculiar course. [5]In two months the moon sets with the sun, in those two middle constellations, the third and fourth constellations. [6]She goes forth for seven days, and turns about and returns again through the portal where the sun rises, and completes all her light; and she recedes from the sun, and in eight days enters the sixth constellation from which the sun goes forth. [7]When the sun comes out from the fourth constellation, she goes forth seven days, until she goes forth from the fifth and turns back again in seven days into the fourth constellation and completes all her light; and she recedes and enters into the first constellation in eight days. [8]She returns again in seven days into the fourth constellation from which the sun goes forth. [9]Thus I saw their positions, the sun and moon rising and setting according to the order of their months.

[10]If five years are taken together, the sun has an excess of thirty[L] days, and all the days for one of those five years, when they are full, amount to three hundred and sixty-four days. [11]The excess of the sun and of the stars amounts to six days. In five years six days per year comes out to be thirty days; and the moon falls behind the sun and stars thirty days. [12]The sun and the stars[M] bring in all the years exactly, so that they do not advance or delay their position by a single day unto eternity; but complete the years with perfect justice in 364 days. [13]In three years there are 1,092 days, and in five years 1,820 days, so that in eight years there are 2,912 days. [14]For the moon alone, three years amounts to 1,062 days, and in five years she falls fifty days behind the sun, to the sum of these are added sixty-two days. [15]In five years there are 1,770 days, so that in eight years the days of the moon will amount to 2,832 days. [16]In eight years she falls behind the sun eighty days; all the days she falls behind in eight years are eighty. [17]The year is accurately completed in conformity with their stations and the stations of the sun, which rise from the constellations through which they rise and set thirty days.

---

[L]  Based on a 360 days. This part of the text has been edited.
[M]  Or "the moon"

# 75 The Four Intercalary Days[N]

The leaders of the heads of the thousands, who are placed over the whole creation and over all the stars, have also to do with the four intercalary days, being inseparable from their office, according to the reckoning of the year; and these render service on the four days which are not counted in the reckoning of the year. [2]On their account men make a mistake in them, for these luminaries truly serve on the stations, one in the first constellation, one in the third constellation, one in the fourth constellation, and one in the sixth constellation; and the exactness of the year is accomplished through its separate three hundred and sixty-four stations. [3]For the signs, times, years, and days the angel Uriel showed to me, whom the Lord of Glory has set forever over all the luminaries of the heaven, in the heaven and in the world, that they should rule on the face of the heaven and be seen on the earth, and be leaders for the day and the night, (the sun, moon, and stars, and all the ministering creatures which make their revolution in all the chariots of the heaven).

## Weather Patterns

[4]Uriel also showed me twelve doors[O] open in the circuit of the sun's chariot in the heaven, through which the rays of the sun break forth, and from them is warmth diffused over the earth, when they are opened at their appointed seasons. [5]There are also some for the winds and the spirit

---

[N] This is the calendar used in Qumran and the book of Jubilees.
[O] How they affect weather patterns.

of the dew when they open at times, standing open in the heavens at the ends.

## The Zodiac and the Decans

[6]As for the twelve constellations in the heaven, at the ends of the earth, out of which go forth the sun, moon, and stars, and all the works of heaven in the east and in the west, [7]there are many decans[P] open to the left and right of them. And one decan comes at its appointed season (the one that produces warmth), corresponding (as these do) to those constellations from which the stars come forth according as He has commanded them, and wherein they set corresponding to their number. [8]I saw chariots in the heaven, running in the world, above those constellations in which revolve the stars that never set.[Q] [9]And one is larger than all the rest, and it is that which makes its course through the entire world.

## 76 *The Four Winds[R]*

*At the ends of the earth I saw twelve portals open to all the quarters (of the heaven), from which the winds go forth and blow over the earth. [2]Three of them are open on the face [east] of the heavens, and three in the west, and three on the right [south] of the heaven, and three on the left [north].*

*[3]The first three are those of the east, and three are of the north, and three (after those on the left) of the*

---

[P] windows
[Q] The north star
[R] This seems to be a re-edited version of chapters 34-36

*south, and three of the west. <sup>4</sup>Through four of these come winds<sup>S</sup> of blessing and prosperity, and from those eight come hurtful winds. When they are sent, they bring destruction on all the earth and on the water upon it, and on all who dwell thereon, and on everything which is in the water and on the land.*

*<sup>5</sup>The first wind from those portals, called the east wind, comes forth through the first portal which is in the east, inclining towards the south. From it come forth destruction, drought, heat, and death. <sup>6</sup>Through the second middle portal comes the right mixture, and from it there comes rain and fruitfulness and prosperity and dew; and through the third portal which lies toward the north come cold and dryness.*

*<sup>7</sup>After these come forth the south winds through three portals. Through the first portal of them inclining to the east comes forth a hot wind. <sup>8</sup>And through the middle portal next to it there come forth fragrant smells, dew, rain, prosperity, and health. <sup>9</sup>Through the third portal lying to the west comes forth dew, rain, locusts, and desolation.*

*<sup>10</sup>After these come the north winds from the seventh portal in the east, inclining to the south. From them come dew, rain, locusts, and desolation. <sup>11</sup>From the*

---

<sup>S</sup> And after these things I saw four angels standing on the four corners of the earth, holding the four winds of the earth, that the wind should not blow on the earth, nor on the sea, nor on any tree. *Revelation 7:1*

middle portal directly comes health, rain, dew, and prosperity; and through the third portal in the west, which inclines toward the north, comes clouds, hoar-frost, snow, rain, dew, and locusts.

[12] *After these four are the west winds. Through the first portal, which inclines toward the north, comes forth dew, rain, hoar-frost[T], cold, snow, and frost. [13] From the middle portal comes forth dew, rain, prosperity, and blessing; and through the last portal, which adjoins the south, comes forth dryness, desolation, burning, and death. [14] Thereby the twelve portals of the four quarters of the heaven are completed, and all their laws and all their plagues and all their benefactions have I shown to you, my son Methuselah.*

# 77 The Quarters

*The first wind[U] is called the east, because it is the first; and the second, the south, because the Most High will descend there, especially the Blessed One will in eternity descend there. [2] The west quarter is named the diminished, because there all the luminaries of the heaven wane and go down. [3] And the fourth quarter, named the north, is divided into three parts: the first of them is for the dwelling of men; and the second contains seas of water, and the abysses, forests, rivers, darkness, and clouds;*

[T] Or locust
[U] Or quarter

*and the third part contains the garden of righteousness.*

*[4]I saw seven high mountains, higher than all the mountains which are on the earth; and there comes forth hoar-frost, and days, seasons, and years pass away. [5]I saw seven rivers on the earth larger than all the rivers. One of them coming from the west pours its waters into the Great Sea. [6]Two come from the north to the sea and empty their waters into the Erythraean Sea in the east. [7]The remaining four come forth on the side of the north to their own sea, two of them to the Erythraean Sea, and two into the Great Sea and discharge themselves there (and some say into the desert). [8]Seven great islands I saw in the sea and in the mainland: two in the mainland and five in the Great Sea.*

78 The names of the sun are these: the first Orjares [shining], and the second Tomas [heat]. [2]The moon has four names: the first name is Asonja, the second Ebla, the third Benase, and the fourth Erae. [3]These are the two great luminaries. Their circuit is like the circuit of the heaven, and they are the same size.[V] [4]In the circuit of the sun there are seven portions of light which are added to it more than to the moon, and in definite measures it is transferred till the seventh portion of the sun is exhausted.[W] [5]They set and enter the constellations of the

[V] The sun and moon look like they are about the same size when looking at them from earth, but they are vastly different.

[W] More heat during certain seasons / constellations.

west, and make their revolution by the north, and come forth through the eastern constellations on the face of the heaven.

[6]When the moon rises, one-fourteenth part appears in the heaven. On the fourteenth day she completes her light. [7]And fifteen parts of light are transferred to her till the fifteenth day when her light is completed, according to the sign of the year, and she becomes fifteen parts, and the moon grows by the addition of fourteenth parts.

[8]On the first day of her waning, she decreases to fourteen parts of her light, on the second to thirteen parts of light, on the third to twelve, on the fourth to eleven, on the fifth to ten, on the sixth to nine, on the seventh to eight, on the eighth to seven, on the ninth to six, on the tenth to five, on the eleventh to four, on the twelfth to three, on the thirteenth to two, on the fourteenth to the half of a seventh, and all her remaining light completely disappears on the fifteenth. [9]And in certain months the month has twenty-nine days, and once twenty-eight.

[10]And Uriel showed me another law: when light is added to the moon, and on which side it is added to her by the sun. [11]During all the period in which the moon is growing in her light, she increases it to herself opposite the sun, till on the fourteenth day her light is completed in the heaven; and when she is fully illumined, her light is completed in the heaven. [12]On the first day she is called the new moon, for on that day the light rises upon her. [13]She becomes a full moon exactly on the day when the sun sets in the

west, and from the east she rises at night, and the moon shines the whole night through till the sun rises opposite her and the moon is seen opposite the sun. [14]On the side whence the light of the moon comes forth, there again she wanes till all the light vanishes and all the days of the month are at an end, and her circumference is empty, void of light. [15]Three months she makes thirty days in her time, and three months she makes twenty-nine days each, in which she completes her waning in the first period of time, and in the first portal for one hundred and seventy-seven days. [16]In the time of her departure she appears for three months of thirty days each, and for three months she appears for twenty-nine days each. [17]At night she appears like a man for twenty days each time, and by day she appears like the heaven, and there is nothing else in her except her light.

79 "Now, my son Methuselah, I have shown you everything, and the law of all the stars of the heaven is completed." [2]He showed me all the laws of these for every day, season, government, and year, and for its going forth, and for the order prescribed to it every month and every week: [3]the waning of the moon which takes place in the sixth portal, for in this sixth portal, her light is accomplished, and after that there is the beginning of the month. [4]The waning which takes place in the first portal, in its season, till one hundred and seventy-seven days are completed, reckoned according to weeks, twenty-five weeks and two days. [5]According to the law of the stars, the moon falls behind the sun exactly five days in the course of one period, and when you see this, its

course will be completed. [6]This is the picture and sketch of each luminary which Uriel the archangel, who is their leader, showed me.

# 80

In those days the angel Uriel answered and said to me, "Behold, I have shown you everything, Enoch, and I have revealed everything to you that you should see in this sun and this moon, and the leaders of the stars of the heaven and all those who turn them, their tasks and times and departures.

## End Time Signs

[2]In the days of the sinners the years will be shortened[X], and their seed will be tardy on their lands and fields, and all things on the earth will alter, and will not appear in their time; and the rain will be kept back and the heaven will retain it. [3]In those times the fruits of the earth will be tardy, and will not grow in their time, and the fruits of the trees will be withheld in their time.[Y] [4]The moon's order will be altered, and not appear at her proper time. [5]In those days the sun will be seen and he will journey in the evening on the extremity of the great chariot in the west and will shine more brightly.[Z] [6]Many chiefs of the stars of

---

[X] And except those days should be shortened, there should no flesh be saved: but for the elect's sake those days shall be shortened. *Matthew 24:22*; See also Proverbs 10:27

[Y] These have power to shut heaven, that it rain not in the days of their prophecy: and have power over waters to turn them to blood, and to smite the earth with all plagues, as often as they will. *Revelation 11:6*

[Z] Moreover the light of the moon shall be as the light of the sun, and the light of the sun shall be sevenfold, as the light of seven days. *Isaiah 30:26*

command will err; these will alter their orbits and tasks, and not appear at the seasons prescribed to them. ⁷The whole order<sup>AA</sup> of the stars will be concealed from the sinners, and the thoughts of those on the earth will err concerning them, and they will be altered from all their ways, and they will err and consider them to be gods.<sup>BB</sup> ⁸Evil will increase upon them, and punishment will come upon them to destroy all."

## 81 Enoch Commanded to Teach

He said unto me, "Enoch, study these heavenly tablets; read what is written on them, and remember every individual fact."

²I studied the heavenly tablets, and read everything which was written on them and understood everything, and read the book of all the deeds of mankind, and of all the children of flesh that will be upon the earth up to the last generation. ³Then I blessed the great Lord, the eternal King of Glory, that He has made all the things of the world; and I exalted the Lord because of His patience, and blessed Him because of the children of men. ⁴After that I said, "Blessed is the man who dies in righteousness and goodness, concerning whom there is no book of unrighteousness written, and against whom no day of judgment will be found."

⁵Those seven holy ones brought me and placed me on the earth before the door of my house, and said to me,

---

AA The science of the Magi will be replaced by pagan astrology.
BB Constellation gods or that humans evolve into gods, or both.

"Declare everything to thy son Methuselah, and show to all thy children that no flesh is righteous in the sight of the Lord[CC], for He is their Creator. [6]One year we will leave you with thy children, till you are strengthened so you can teach your children and record it for them, and testify to all thy children; and in the second year you will be lifted up out of their presence. [7]Be strong in heart, for the good will announce righteousness to the good; the righteous with the righteous will rejoice, and will offer congratulation to one another. [8]But the sinners will die with the sinners, and the apostate go down with the apostate. [9]Those who practice righteousness will die on account of the deeds of men, and be taken away on account of the doings of the godless. [10]In those days they ceased to speak to me, and I came to my people, blessing the Lord of the world."

# 82 Enoch Returns to His Family

Now, my son Methuselah, all these things I have recounted and written down for you! I have revealed to you everything, and given you books concerning all these. So preserve, my son Methuselah, the books from your father's hand, and see that you deliver them to the generations of the world. [2]I have given wisdom to you, and to your children, and those who will be your children, that they may give it to their children for generations; this

---

[CC] Knowing that a man is not justified by the works of the law, but by the faith of Jesus Christ, even we have believed in Jesus Christ, that we might be justified by the faith of Christ, and not by the works of the law: for by the works of the law shall no flesh be justified. *Galatians 2:16*

wisdom that surpasses their understanding[DD]. [3]Those who understand it will not sleep, but will listen with the ear that they may learn this wisdom, and it will please those that eat thereof better than good food. [4]Blessed are all the righteous. Blessed are all those who walk in the way of righteousness and sin not as the sinners, in the reckoning of all their days in which the sun traverses the heaven, entering into and departing from the portals for thirty days with the heads of thousands of the order of the stars, together with the four which are intercalated which divide the four portions of the year, which lead them and enter with them four days. [5]Owing to them, men will be at fault and not reckon them in the whole reckoning of the year; but men will be mistaken, and not recognize them accurately. [6]For they belong to the reckoning of the year and are truly recorded forever, one in the first portal and one in the third, and one in the fourth and one in the sixth, and the year is completed in three hundred and sixty-four days. [7]This account is accurate and the recorded reckoning thereof exact; for the luminaries, and months and festivals, and years, and days; and Uriel has shown and revealed to me, to whom the Lord of the whole creation of the world has subjected the host of heaven. [8]He has power over night and day in the heaven to give the light: the sun, moon, stars, and all the powers of the heaven, which revolve in their circuits. [9]These are the

---

[DD] And the peace of God, which passeth all understanding, shall keep your hearts and minds through Christ Jesus. *Philippians 4:7*

orders of the stars, which set in their places, and in their seasons, festivals[EE], and months.

[10]These are the names of those who lead them, who watch that they enter at their times, in their orders, in their seasons, in their months, in their periods of dominion, and in their positions. [11]Their four leaders who divide the four parts of the year enter first; and after them the twelve leaders of the orders who divide the months; and for the three hundred and sixty-four days, together with the heads over thousands who divide the days, and for the four intercalary days there are the leaders which separate the four parts of the year. [12]Of these heads over thousands, one is placed between the leader and the led, each behind a station, but their leaders make the division.

[13]These are the names of the leaders who divide the four parts of the year which are ordained: Melkiel, Helemmelek, and Meleial, and Narel. [14]The names of those whom they lead: Adnarel, and Iyasusael, and Iyelumiel. These three follow the leaders of the orders, and there is one who follows the three leaders of the orders which follow those leaders of stations that divide the four parts of the year.

[15]In the beginning of the year Melkiel rises first and rules, who is called Tamaani. And the sun, and all the days of his dominion while he bears rule, are ninety-one days. [16]And these are the signs of the days which are to be seen

---

[EE] Study the rituals of the messianic festivals and the star patterns in the months they represent; e.g. Tishrei for Yom Kippur.

on earth in the days of his dominion: sweat, and heat, and calm; and all the trees bear fruit, and leaves are produced on all the trees, and the harvest of wheat, and the roses, and all the flowers which come forth in the field, but the trees of the winter season become withered. [17]And these are the names of the leaders which are under them: Berkael, Zelbesael, and another who is added, a head of a thousand, called Heloyaseph; and the days of the dominion of this one are at an end.

[18]The next leader after him is Helemmelek, who is called the shining sun, and all the days of his light are ninety-one days. [19]These are the signs of the days on the earth: burning heat, dryness, and the trees ripen, then produce their fruits, and the sheep mate and become pregnant, and all the fruits of the earth are gathered in, and everything that is in the fields, and the winepress; these things take place in the days of his dominion. [20]These are the names, and the orders, and the leaders of those heads of thousands: Gedael, Keel, and Heel, and the name of the head of a thousand which is added to them, Asphael, and the days of his dominion are at an end.

## Commentary

The description of the calendar is given describing the constellation the sun is in when it rises and which constellation is setting in the west at that time. E.g. the sun rising in the first eastern portal (Aries) while the first western portal (Libra) sets.

| Gregorian | Hebrew | Sun rises in | Western horizon |
|-----------|--------|--------------|-----------------|
| April | Nisan | Aries | Libra |
| May | Iyar | Taurus | Scorpio |
| June | Sivan | Gemini | Sagittarius |
| July | Tammuz | Cancer | Capricorn |
| August | Av | Leo | Aquarius |
| September | Elul | Virgo | Pisces |
| October | Tishrei | Libra | Aries |
| November | Cheshvan | Scorpio | Taurus |
| December | Kislev | Sagittarius | Gemini |
| January | Tevet | Capricorn | Cancer |
| February | Shevat | Aquarius | Leo |
| March | Adar | Pisces | Virgo |

# First Dream - The Flood 83-84

## 83 Dream of the Flood

My son, Methuselah, I will reveal to you all my visions which I have seen. ²I had two visions before I took a wife, and the two were vastly different. The first [occurred] when I was just learning to write, and the second was right before I married your mother. I was awestruck by them, so I continued to pray to the Lord about them.

³I had just lain down in my grandfather Mahalalel's house, when I saw the heavens collapse[A] and fall to the earth. ⁴This caused the earth to be swallowed up in a great abyss. Mountains were suspended on mountains, hills sank down on hills, and high trees were ripped up from the ground and hurled into the abyss. ⁵I suddenly cried out loud from my sleep, "the earth is destroyed!"

⁶Grandfather Mahalalel woke me as I lay near him, and said unto me, "What is wrong, my son?" ⁷I recounted to him the whole vision, and he said unto me, "It is a terrible thing you have seen, my son, — this vision has to do with the secrets of all the sin of the earth. It must sink into the abyss and be destroyed. ⁸My son, since you are a believer,

---

[A] In the six hundredth year of Noah's life, in the second month, the seventeenth day of the month, the same day were all the fountains of the great deep broken up, and the windows of heaven were opened. And the rain was upon the earth forty days and forty nights. *Genesis 7:11-12*

arise and pray to the Lord of Glory not to destroy the whole earth, but to leave a remnant. [9]My son, a great destruction from heaven will come over all the earth."

[10]So I arose and prayed and wrote down my prayer for the generations of the world, and I will show everything to you, my son Methuselah. [11]After I went out below, I saw the sun rise in the east, the moon set in the west, a few stars, and the earth as it was before. Then I blessed the Lord because His creation was just as it was. The sun rose and set as before.

# 84 Prayer For Forgiveness

I lifted my hands and blessed the Lord with the breath of my mouth and the tongue of my flesh which the Lord has created for men to do, saying, "[2]Blessed are You, O Lord, King, great and mighty, Lord of the whole creation of the heaven, King of kings and God of the whole world. Your power, kingship, and greatness will abide forever; Your dominion throughout all generations; Your throne and all the heavens forever; the whole earth as Your footstool forever. [3]For You have made and rule all things; nothing is too hard for You. Wisdom never departs from Your throne nor Your presence. You know, see, and hear everything. There is nothing hidden from You. [4]The angels of Your heavens are guilty of trespass and Your wrath abides upon the flesh of men until the great day of judgment. [5]O God and Lord, I implore You, hear my prayer! Leave me a posterity on earth. Do not destroy all mankind, making the earth without inhabitant.

Do not make this destruction eternal.[B] [6]My Lord, destroy the flesh which has angered You from the earth, but the flesh of righteousness establish as a plant of the eternal seed. Do not hide Your face from the prayer of Your servant, O Lord."

---

[B] He never asks God to stop the coming destruction, but to allow a remnant.

# Second Dream 85-90

## 85 Adam, Eve, Cain, and Abel

After this I saw another dream which I will now reveal to you. [2]My son, listen carefully to my second dream that I had before I married your mother, Edna. [3]I dreamed a white bull [Adam] came up out of the earth; and after it came up a heifer [Eve], and along with the heifer came up a black bull [Cain] and a red bull [Abel]. [4]The black bull gored the red one and chased him away to the point I could no longer see that red bull. [5]Then the black bull grew and the heifer[A] went with him, and he produced many oxen which resembled him and followed him. [6]Then that cow left the first bull to find the red one, but she couldn't find him and lamented greatly but kept looking for him. [7]I looked till that first bull came to her and quieted her, and from that time onward she cried no more.

### Seth

[8]After that she bore another white bull [Seth], and after him she bore many bulls and black cows. [9]The white bull then grew and became a great white bull, and he produced many white bulls, and they resembled him. [10]They began to beget many white bulls which resembled them, one after another.

---

[A] When Cain was banished to the Land of Nod he took one of his sisters, Awan, with him for a wife. See Jubilees 4:9 and Josephus 1.2.1

# 86 The Creation of the Nephilim

Then I saw a star [Azazel] fall from heaven, and it arose and ate and pastured among the cows. [2]After that I saw the large cows [Sethites] and the black cows [Cainites], and they changed their stalls, pastures, and their young began to cry against each other. [3]I looked towards the heaven, and behold I saw many stars descend from heaven[B] and bowed down to that first star, and they became bulls among those cattle and pastured among them. [4]Then they let out their sexual organs, like horses do, and mounted and impregnated the cows and the cows bore elephants, camels, and asses[C]. [5]All the cattle feared them, and began to bite with their teeth and to devour, and to gore with their horns. [6]They began to devour those cattle; and behold all the children of the earth began to tremble and quake before them and to flee from them.

# 87 Enoch's Translation

Then as they were goring one another the earth began to cry aloud. [2]I looked up to heaven and saw beings who looked like white men coming down from heaven. The first one [Michael] went forth from that heaven, then the other three [archangels] followed him. [3]The last three came and took me by the hand to a high tower, far away from the children of the earth [Enoch's Rapture]. [4]One

---

[B] And the angels which kept not their first estate, but left their own habitation, he hath reserved in everlasting chains under darkness unto the judgment of the great day. *Jude 1:6*;

[C] Three different clans of Nephilim - They begat sons, the Nâphîdîm, and they were all unlike, and they devoured one another: and the Giants slew the Nâphîl, and the Nâphîl slew the Eliô [Elioud], and the Eliô, mankind, and one man another. *Jubilees 7:22*

told me, "Remain here until you see everything that happens to all the elephants, camels, and asses, and the stars and the cattle."

# 88 The Nephilim Civil War

Then one of those first four [Raphael[D]] seized that first star which had fallen from the heaven [Azazel] and bound it hand and foot and cast it into an abyss. Now that abyss was narrow, deep, horrible, and dark. [2]One of the other four [Gabriel] drew a sword, and gave it to those elephants, camels, and asses. Then they began to smite each other, and the whole earth shook because of them.[E] [3]Then one of those first four [Michael] gathered all the great stars whose sexual organs portrayed like horses, and bound them all hand and foot, and cast them in an abyss of the earth.[F]

# 89 The Flood

One of those four went to that white bull [Noah] and instructed him in a secret, while it was terrified. He was born a bull but became a man, and built a great vessel and dwelt in it. Three bulls [Ham, Shem, and Japheth] dwelt with him in that vessel which covered them. [2]I looked up to heaven and saw a high roof with seven water torrents. A great amount of water flowed through those torrents into an enclosure. [3]As I was watching, fountains

---

[D] Enoch 10

[E] The Nephilim civil war. See Jubilees 7:22

[F] For if God spared not the angels that sinned, but cast them down to hell, and delivered them into chains of darkness, to be reserved unto judgment; *2 Peter 2:4*

were opened on the surface of that great enclosure, and that water began to swell and rise upon the surface, and I watched that enclosure till all its surface was covered with water. [4]The water, darkness, and mist kept increasing. The water rose above the height of that enclosure, and streamed over the sides and poured upon the whole earth. [5]All the cattle gathered together, but eventually they were swallowed up and perished in that water.

[6]But the vessel floated upon the water while *all* the cattle, elephants, camels, and asses, along with *all* the animals, sank to the bottom so that I could no longer see them. They were not able to escape, but perished into the depths.[G] [7]Then the water torrents were removed from that high roof and the chasms of the earth were levelled up and other abysses were opened. [8]Then the water began to run down into these abysses till the earth became visible, and that vessel settled on the earth, and the darkness retired and light appeared.

[9]But that white bull [Noah] which had become a man came out of that vessel, and the three bulls with him, and one of those three was white [Shem] like that bull [Noah], and one of them was red [Japheth] as blood, and one black [Ham];[H] and that white bull [Noah] departed from them.[I]

---

[G] None of the pre-flood humans or Nephilim survived the Flood.

[H] Shem was godly and Ham turned evil.

[I] Legend says Noah retired to the island of Crete and experimented with various ship designs. At his death he was taken back and buried by the Ark.

[10]They began to bring forth beasts of the field and birds, so that there arose different species [Gentile nations]: lions, tigers, wolves, dogs, hyenas, wild boars, foxes, squirrels, swine, falcons, vultures, kites, eagles, and ravens; and among them was born a white bull [Abraham].

## Abraham to Joseph

[11]They began to bite one another; but that white bull [Abraham] which was born among them begat a wild ass [Ishmael] and a white bull [Isaac] with it, and the wild asses [Arab nations] multiplied. [12]But that bull which was born from him begat a black wild boar [Esau] and a white sheep [Jacob / Israel]; and the former begat many boars, but that sheep begat twelve sheep [twelve tribes of Israel]. [13]When those twelve sheep had grown, they gave up one of them to the asses [Ishmaelite slave traders], and those asses again gave up that sheep [Joseph] to the wolves[J] [Egyptians], and that sheep grew up among the wolves. [14]And the Lord brought the eleven sheep to live with it and to pasture with it among the wolves; and they multiplied and became many flocks of sheep. [15]The wolves began to fear them, and they oppressed them until they killed their little ones, and they cast their young into a great river of water [Nile River]; but those sheep began to cry aloud on account of their little ones, and to complain unto their Lord.

---

[J] Aramaic has "bears" instead of "wolves."

## Moses

[16]A sheep [Moses] which had been saved from the wolves fled and escaped to the wild asses [Midianites]; and I saw the sheep how they lamented and cried, and besought their Lord with all their might, till the Lord of the sheep [Yahweh] descended at the voice of the sheep from a lofty abode, and came to them and pastured them. [17]He called that sheep which had escaped the wolves, and spoke with it concerning the wolves that it should warn them not to touch the sheep. [18]The sheep went to the wolves according to the word of the Lord, and another sheep met it and went with it, and the two [Moses and Aaron] went together and entered into the assembly of those wolves, and spoke with them and warned them not to touch the sheep any longer. [19]Then I saw the wolves, and how they greatly oppressed the sheep with all their power; and the sheep cried aloud. [20]The Lord came to the sheep and they began to smite those wolves [the ten plagues]; and the wolves began to make lamentation, but the sheep became quiet and ceased crying out.

## The Exodus

[21]The sheep departed from the wolves [the Exodus]; but the eyes of the wolves were blinded, and those wolves pursued the sheep with all their power. [22]And the Lord of the sheep [Yahweh] went with them, as their leader, and all His sheep followed Him; and His face was dazzling and glorious to behold. [23]But the wolves began to pursue those sheep till they reached a sea of water [Red Sea]. [24]And that sea was divided, and the water stood on both sides right before their eyes, and their Lord led them and

stood between them and the wolves. [25]Even though those wolves could not see the sheep, they preceded into the midst of that sea, following the sheep. [26]When they saw the Lord of the sheep [Yahweh], they turned to flee, but that sea gathered itself together, and became as it had been created, [27]and the water drowned those wolves. [28]But the sheep escaped from that water and travelled into a wilderness where there was no water or grass, and they began to open their eyes and see; and I saw the Lord of the sheep [Yahweh] pasturing them and giving them water and grass, and that sheep [Moses] going and leading them. [29]And that sheep ascended to the summit of that lofty rock [Moses on Mt. Sinai], and the Lord of the sheep sent it to them.

## Moses and Mt. Sinai

[30]After that I saw the Lord of the sheep who stood before them, and His appearance was great, terrible, and majestic; and all those sheep saw Him and were afraid before His face. [31]They all feared and trembled because of Him, and they cried to that sheep with them, "We are not able to stand before our Lord or to behold Him." [32]Then that sheep which led them again ascended to the summit of that rock, but the sheep began to be blinded and to wander from the way which he had showed them, but that sheep did not know it. [33]The Lord of the sheep was enraged at them, and that sheep [Moses] discovered it, and went down from the summit of the rock, and came to the sheep, and found the greatest part of them blinded and fallen away. [34]When they saw it, they feared and trembled at its presence, and desired to return to their folds. [35]And

that sheep took other sheep with it, and came to those sheep which had fallen away, and began to slay them; and the sheep feared its presence, and thus that sheep brought back those sheep that had fallen away, and they returned to their folds.

## Forty Years in the Wilderness

[36]Then I saw in this vision till that sheep [Moses] became a man and built a house [nation of Israel] for the Lord of the sheep, and placed all the sheep in that house. [37]And I saw till this sheep which had met that sheep which led them died [forty years in the wilderness]. And I saw till all the great sheep died and little ones arose in their place, and they came to a pasture, and approached a stream of water [Jordan River]. [38]Then that sheep, their leader which had become a man [Moses], withdrew from them and died and all the sheep sought it and cried over it greatly. [39]I saw till they stopped crying for that sheep and crossed that stream of water [Jordan River], and there arose the other sheep as leaders in the place of those which had led them and fallen asleep [Joshua and the Judges]. [40]The sheep came to a good place, a pleasant and glorious land, and I saw till those sheep were satisfied; and that house stood amongst them in the pleasant land [Israel].

## Judges Period

[41]And sometimes their eyes were opened, and sometimes blinded, till another sheep arose and led them and brought them all back, and their eyes were opened.

## Saul

[42]The dogs [Philistines], foxes [Ammonites and Moabites], and wild boars [Edom and Amalek] began to devour those sheep till the Lord of the sheep raised up a ram [King Saul] from their midst, which led them. [43]And that ram began to butt those dogs, foxes, and wild boars till he had destroyed them all. [44]And that sheep [Samuel the Prophet] whose eyes were opened, saw that ram (which was amongst the sheep) till it forsook its glory and began to butt those sheep, and trampled upon them, and behaved itself unseemly.

## David

[45]The Lord of the sheep sent the sheep [Samuel the Prophet] to a lamb and raised it to be a ram [David] and leader of the sheep instead of that ram which had forsaken its glory. [46]It went to it and spoke to it alone, and raised it to be a ram, and made it the prince and leader of the sheep; but during all these things those dogs [Philistines] oppressed the sheep. [47]The first ram [Saul] pursued that second ram [David], and that second ram arose and fled before it; and I saw till those dogs pulled down the first ram. [48]That second ram [David] arose and led the sheep. [49]Those sheep grew and multiplied; but all the dogs [Philistines], foxes [Ammonites and Moabites], and wild boars [Edom and Amalek] feared and fled from him. That ram butted and killed the wild beasts. That ram begat many sheep and fell asleep; and

## Solomon

a little sheep [Solomon] became a prince and leader of those sheep. [50]That house [nation of Israel] became great and broad, and it was built for those sheep; and a great and lofty tower [Solomon's Temple] was built on the house for the Lord of the sheep, and that house was low, but the tower was elevated and lofty, and the Lord of the sheep stood on that tower and they offered a full table before Him.

## The Prophets

[51]Those sheep again erred and went many ways, and forsook their house. And the Lord of the sheep called some from amongst the sheep [the prophets] and sent them to the sheep, but the sheep began to slay them.

## Elijah

[52]One of them [Elijah] was saved and was not slain, and it sped away and cried aloud over the sheep, and they sought to kill it; but the Lord of the sheep saved it from the sheep, and brought it up to me [raptured], and caused it to dwell there. [53]He sent many other sheep [prophets] to those sheep [northern tribes] to testify unto them and lament over them.

## Kings of Israel and Judah

[54]After that I saw that when they forsook the house of the Lord and His tower, they fell away entirely, and their eyes were blinded; and I saw the Lord of the sheep how He wrought much slaughter amongst them in their herds until those sheep invited that slaughter and betrayed His place.

## Assyria and Babylon

[55]He gave them over into the hands of the lions and tigers [Assyria and Babylon?][K], wolves and hyenas, and into the hand of the foxes and wild beasts, and those wild beasts began to tear those sheep into pieces. [56]I saw that Yahweh left the house and the tower [Solomon's Temple] and gave it all into the hands of the lions [Babylon] that they should tear down and destroy them. [57]I began to cry aloud with all my power, and to appeal to the Lord of the sheep in regard to the sheep. [58]But He remained unmoved, though He saw it, and rejoiced that they were devoured, swallowed, and robbed. He left them in the hands of those beasts for food.

## The Seventy Shepherds

[59]He called seventy shepherds, and gave the care of the sheep over to them. He said to the shepherds and their companions, "Let each one of you pasture the sheep and do everything exactly as I command you. [60]I will deliver them over unto you duly numbered, and tell you which of them you are to destroy." [61]When He had given the sheep over unto them, He called to another [Michael] and said, "Write down everything that the shepherds do to those sheep; for they will destroy more of them than I have commanded. [62]Record how many they destroy out of the ones I command them to destroy and how many out of the ones I command them not to destroy. Record against every individual shepherd all the destruction he effects, [63]so that I may have this as a testimony against them, and

---

[K] Assyria destroyed the northern tribes in 722 BC; Babylon destroyed Judah in 607 BC and burnt the temple in 587 BC.

know every deed of the shepherds, whether or not they abide by My command which I have commanded them. [64]Do not declare it to them, nor warn them, but only record against each individual all the destruction which the shepherds effect each in his time and lay it all before Me."

## Rehoboam to Zedekiah

[65]I saw till those shepherds pastured for a season, and they began to kill and to destroy more than they were bidden, and they delivered those sheep into the hand of the lions. [66]The lions and tigers [Assyrians and Babylonians] ate and devoured the greater part of those sheep, and the wild boars [Edomites?] ate along with them; and they burnt that tower[L] [Solomon's Temple] and demolished that house [Kingdom of Judah]. [67]I mourned a great deal over that tower because the house of the sheep was demolished, and afterwards I was unable to see if those sheep entered that house.[M]

| 1 | Rehoboam |
|---|---|
| 2 | Abijam |
| 3 | Asa |
| 4 | Jehoshaphat |
| 5 | Jehoram |
| 6 | Ahaziah |
| 7 | Athaliah (Q) |
| 8 | Joash |
| 9 | Amaziah |
| 10 | Azariah |
| 11 | Jotham |
| 12 | Ahaziah |
| 13 | Hezekiah |
| 14 | Manasseh |
| 15 | Amon |
| 16 | Josiah |
| 17 | Jehoahaz |
| 18 | Jehoiakim |
| 19 | Jehoiachin |
| 20 | Zedekiah |

[68]It was written by the other [Michael] in a book, how many each one of them destroyed of them. [69]Each one killed and destroyed many more than he was ordered; and

---

[L] Nebuchadnezzar burned the Temple in 587 BC.
[M] Israel was not in their land, but in captivity in Babylon.

I began to weep for those sheep. [70]I watched how he wrote down every one that was destroyed by those shepherds, day by day, and carried up and showed the whole book to the Lord, everything that they had done. [71]The book was read before the Lord, and He took the book from his hand and read it, sealed it, and laid it down.

## The 12 Hours - Babylon to Antiochus Epiphanes

[72]I saw how the shepherds pastured for twelve hours[N], and behold, three of those sheep turned back and came and entered and began to build up all that had fallen down of that house [Zerubbabel, Ezra, and Nehemiah]. The wild boars [Edomites and Arabs] tried to hinder them, but they were not able. [73]They built up that tower, and it was named the high tower [the second temple]. Then they began again to place a table [sacrifices and worship] before the tower, but all the bread on it was polluted and not pure [Antiochus Epiphanes].[O] [74]All the sheep, as well as the shepherds, were blind to all this and a great number of the sheep were delivered to their shepherds for

---

[N] There were two breaks when the shepherds themselves were out to pasture. After the first twenty ruled, there is a break of eleven Gentile powers; then the next fourteen shepherds ruled. The last break was Rome's rule until the last thirty-fifth shepherd ruled. The twelve times (Gentile kingdoms) passed over the sheep. See *Ancient Book of Daniel* pp. 190-121 for details on each successive empire and their respective dates.

[O] Antiochus Epiphanes defiled the second temple by sacrificing a pig on the altar. It was desolate for three years. Then the Maccabees regained control of Israel and rededicated the temple. This is commemorated in the festival of Hanukah. See *Ancient Messianic Festivals* for further information.

destruction. And they trampled the sheep with their feet and devoured them.

### The 12 Hours of Gentile Powers

| 1 | Babylonian Empire | Nebuchadnezzar |
|----|-------------------|----------------------|
| 2 | Persian Empire | Cyrus |
| 3 | Grecian Empire | Alexander the Great |
| 4 | Ptolemaic Empire | Ptolemy I |
| 5 | Seleucid Empire | Antiochus II |
| 6 | Ptolemaic Empire | Ptolemy III |
| 7 | Seleucid Empire | Seleucus III |
| 8 | Ptolemaic Empire | Ptolemy IV |
| 9 | Seleucid Empire | Antiochus III |
| 10 | Ptolemaic Empire | Ptolemy V |
| 11 | Seleucid Empire | Antiochus Epiphanes |

**Maccabean Gap**

| 12 | Roman Empire | Caesar |
|----|--------------|--------|

## The Maccabean Rule to Roman

[75]The Lord of the sheep remained unmoved till all the sheep were dispersed[P] over the field and mingled with the beasts, and the shepherds did not save them out of the hand of the beasts. [76]The one who wrote the book carried it up, and read it before the Lord, and implored Him on their account, showing all the things the shepherds did. [77]He took the actual book and laid it down beside Him and departed. [Gospel age began at this time.]

| 21 | Judah Macabee |
|----|---------------|
| 22 | John |
| 23 | Simon |
| 24 | John |
| 25 | Judah |
| 26 | Alexander |
| 27 | Shalenit |
| 28 | Aristobulus |
| 29 | Hyrekanos |
| 30 | Antigonus |
| 31 | Herod |
| 32 | Archelaus |
| 33 | Agrippa I |
| 34 | Agrippa II |

---

[P] Roman dispersion, AD 132-1948

# 90 Last of the Thirty-five
I watched till in this manner
the thirty-five[R] shepherds pastured

| Rome[Q] |
|---|
| 35 Bar Kokhba |

the sheep; and they each completed their period as did the first, one after the other, each shepherd in his own period.

## Roman Dispersion After Bar Kokhba AD 132-1948

[2]After that I saw in my vision all the birds of heaven coming, eagles [Rome], vultures, kites, ravens; but the eagles led all the birds; and they began to devour those sheep, and to pick out their eyes and to devour their flesh. [3]And the sheep cried out because their flesh was being devoured by the birds. And as for me, I looked and cried out in my sleep over that shepherd who pastured the sheep. [4]And I watched until those sheep were devoured by the dogs and eagles and kites, and they did not leave any flesh, skin, or sinew on them, only their bones stood there.[S] And their bones, too, fell to the earth and the sheep became very few in number.

---

[Q] Rome took control of Israel in 65 BC, but allowed them to have their own kings. After the thirty-fourth shepherd, Agrippa II, Israel was without a king. The temple was destroyed in AD 70. In AD 132, Simon Bar Kokhba led a rebellion that resulted in a three-year independent state of Israel. The Romans finally crushed and dispersed the Jews, fulfilling the prophecies of Micah 5 and Daniel 11.

[R] Some texts have thirty-six or thirty-seven shepherds, but only thirty-five goes along with the count of the seventy shepherds.

[S] Ezekiel 37 = The valley of dry bones

## Modern Israel - The Twenty-three

[5]I watched the next twenty-three[T] shepherds pastured, but when they completed their periods, they had pastured fifty-eight times[U] [Gospel age will close when these are complete].

## Note on the Twenty-three Shepherds

These have to be interpreted in one of three ways:

1. There will be twenty-three Prime Ministers who occupy fifty-eight terms of office, some being re-elected. Currently, there have been thirteen Prime Ministers out of twenty-one terms of office.[V]
2. There will be twenty-three Prime Ministers in fifty-eight Israeli governments. Currently, there have been thirteen Prime Ministers out of thirty-two Israeli governments.
3. There will be twenty-three terms in fifty-eight governments. Currently, there have been twenty-one terms out of thirty-two governments.

---

[T] After the Roman dispersion (AD 132-1948), the middle twenty-three shepherds begin to rule.

[U] These could be figured as twenty-three Prime Ministers in fifty-eight separate terms or governments. These could also be figured as twenty-three prime ministers or twenty-three terms in fifty-eight governments.

[V] Menachem Begin served two consecutive terms. Ariel Sharon served a term plus a 100-day period of "temporary incapacitation" wherein the Prime Minister's authorities were delegated to the Designated Acting Prime Minister. Ehud Olmert served one term, and, in addition, served as Acting Prime Minister, wherein the Prime Minister's authorities were delegated to him.

The most literal interpretation would be twenty-three Prime Ministers in fifty-eight terms.

According to wikipedia.com, as of AD 2012, there have been thirteen men ruling twenty-one terms of office for thirty-two governments in sixty-four years. The lists are given here. Add to them as time goes by and figure out how to properly interpret this prophecy.

| Term | Name | Shepherd |
|------|------|----------|
| 1 | David Ben-Gurion | 1 |
| 2 | Mose Sharett | 2 |
| 3 | David Ben-Gurion | |
| 4 | Levi Eshkol | 3 |
| 5 | Yigal Allon | 4 |
| 6 | Golda Meir | 5 |
| 7 | Yitzhak Rabin | 6 |
| 8-9 | Menachem Begin | 7 |
| 10 | Yitzhak Shamir | 8 |
| 11 | Shimon Peres | 9 |
| 12 | Yitzhak Shamir | |
| 13 | Yitzhak Rabin | |
| 14 | Shimon Peres | |
| 15 | Benjamin Netanyahu | 10 |
| 16 | Ehud Barak | 11 |
| 17-18 | Ariel Sharon | 12 |
| 19-20 | Ehud Olmert | 13 |
| 21 | Benjamin Netanyahu | |
| 22 | | |
| 23 | | |

Write the names, shepherds, and terms in this book when they occur, to estimate how much time is left in our present age.

| Term | Name | Shepherd |
|------|------|----------|
| 24 | | |
| 25 | | |
| 26 | | |
| 27 | | |
| 28 | | |
| 29 | | |
| 30 | | |
| 31 | | |
| 32 | | |
| 33 | | |
| 34 | | |
| 35 | | |
| 36 | | |
| 37 | | |
| 38 | | |
| 39 | | |
| 40 | | |
| 41 | | |
| 42 | | |
| 43 | | |
| 44 | | |
| 45 | | |
| 46 | | |
| 47 | | |
| 48 | | |
| 49 | | |
| 50 | | |
| 51 | | |
| 52 | | |
| 53 | | |
| 54 | | |
| 55 | | |
| 56 | | |
| 57 | | |
| 58 | | |

## Israeli Governments

| | | | |
|---|---|---|---|
| 1. | March 8, 1949 | 30. | February 28, 2003 |
| 2. | November 1, 1950 | 31. | May 4, 2006 |
| 3. | October 8, 1951 | 32. | March 31, 2009 |
| 4. | December 24, 1952 | 33. | |
| 5. | January 26, 1954 | 34. | |
| 6. | June 29, 1955 | 35. | |
| 7. | November 3, 1955 | 36. | |
| 8. | January 7, 1958 | 37. | |
| 9. | December 17, 1959 | 38. | |
| 10. | November 2, 1961 | 39. | |
| 11. | June 26, 1963 | 40. | |
| 12. | December 22, 1964 | 41. | |
| 13. | January 12, 1966 | 42. | |
| 14. | March 17, 1969 | 43. | |
| 15. | December 15, 1969 | 44. | |
| 16. | March 10, 1974 | 45. | |
| 17. | June 3, 1974 | 46. | |
| 18. | June 20, 1977 | 47. | |
| 19. | August 5, 1981 | 48. | |
| 20. | October 10, 1983 | 49. | |
| 21. | September 13, 1984 | 50. | |
| 22. | October 20, 1986 | 51. | |
| 23. | December 22, 1988 | 52. | |
| 24. | June 11, 1990 | 53. | |
| 25. | July 13, 1992 | 54. | |
| 26. | November 22, 1995 | 55. | |
| 27. | June 18, 1996 | 56. | |
| 28. | July 6, 1999 | 57. | |
| 29. | March 7, 2001 | 58. | |

Israeli Governments listed are from Wikipedia.com.

## Messianic vs. Orthodox and Secular

[6]But behold lambs [messianic Jews] were borne by those white sheep [orthodox Jews], and they began to open their eyes and to see, and to cry to the sheep [Orthodox and secular]. [7]The lambs cried to them, but the sheep would not listen; they were completely deaf and blinded to what was told to them.

## A Future Messianic Leader[A]

[8]I saw in the vision how the ravens [Muslims] flew upon those lambs and took one of those lambs [a future messianic leader], and dashed the sheep in pieces and devoured them. [9]And I saw till horns grew upon those lambs, and the ravens cast down their horns;

## Messianic Judaism becomes the Norm

and I saw a great horn sprouted out on one of those sheep, and their eyes were opened. [10]And it looked at them, and their eyes opened, and it cried to the sheep, and the rams saw it and all ran to it.

## Persecution turns toward the Messianic Jews

[11]And, notwithstanding all this, those eagles, vultures, ravens, and kites still kept tearing the sheep and swooping down upon them and devouring them. Still the sheep remained silent, but the rams lamented and cried out.

---

[A] Either this refers to an assassination of a prominent Messianic Rabbi, or a prominent Messianic Rabbi is taken by Muslims and becomes the Antichrist.

135

[12]And those ravens fought and battled with it and sought to lay low its horn, but they had no power over it.[B]

## The Remnant Flee to Petra

[13]All the [last twelve] shepherds[C] and eagles, vultures, and kites came and cried to the ravens, that they should break the horn of the ram. It fought with them and cried out that help might come. [14]I saw that man come, who had written down the names of the shepherds [Michael] and brought them to the Lord of the sheep, and he helped the ram and showed him everything. Its help [Judgment] was coming down.

## God's Wrath - Last 3.5 Years

[15]The Lord of the sheep came to them in anger, and everyone who saw Him fled, and all fell into His shadow before His face. [16]The eagles, vultures, ravens, and kites assembled together with all the desert sheep. They all came together and assisted one another in order to break the horn of the ram.

## The Twelve Shepherds of the Seven-Year Tribulation

[17]I saw that man who wrote the book according to the command of the Lord, till he opened that book of destruction, the destruction which those twelve last shepherds had done, and showed that they had destroyed much more than their predecessors, before the Lord of the

---

[B] Antichrist has no power in Jordan where the believers flee to the city of Petra; see Daniel 11:41.

[C] Secular Jews side with the Antichrist in his persecution of the Messianic believers.

sheep. [18]The Lord of the sheep came unto them and took the staff of His wrath in His hand, and smote the earth, and the earth was torn apart, and all the beasts and all the birds of the heaven fell away from those sheep, and were swallowed up in the earth and it covered them.

[19]Then a great sword was given to the sheep, and the sheep proceeded against all the beasts of the field to kill them, and all the beasts and the birds of the heaven fled before their face.[D]

## Millennial Reign
[20]I watched till a throne was erected in the pleasant land [Israel], and the Lord of the sheep [Ancient of Days] sat on it; and He [The Messiah] took all of the sealed books[E] and opened those books before the Lord of the sheep.

[21]The Lord called to those first seven white ones, and commanded them to bring the first star [Azazel?] before Him, who in the beginning caused the fall of all the stars, who let out their sexual organs like horses, and they brought the first star first, then all the others before Him.

[22]He said to that man [Michael] who wrote before Him, being one of those seven white ones, and said unto him, "Of those seventy shepherds to whom I delivered the sheep, bring those who took them on their own authority

---

[D] But the saints of the most High shall take the kingdom, and possess the kingdom forever, even forever and ever. *Daniel 7:18*
[E] Revelation 4-5

and killed more than I commanded them." [23]Behold they were all bound, I saw, and they all stood before Him.

## Judgment of the Stars

[24]The judgment was held first over the stars, and they were judged and found guilty, and went to the place of condemnation. And they were cast into an abyss full of fire, flames, and pillars of fire.

## Judgment of the Seventy Shepherds

[25]Those of the seventy shepherds who were bound before the Lord were judged, found guilty, and were cast into that fiery abyss. [26]I saw at that time how a similar abyss was opened in the middle of the earth[F], full of fire, and they brought those blinded sheep, and they were all judged and found guilty and cast into this fiery abyss, and burned. Now this abyss [Gehenna[G]] was to the right [south] of that house [Jerusalem]. [27]I saw those sheep burning and their bones burning.

## Millennial Temple

[28]I stood up to see till they folded up that old house and carried off all the pillars, beams, and the ornaments of the house were at the same time folded up with it, and they carried it off and laid it in a place in the south of the land. [29]I saw till the Lord of the sheep created a new larger and higher house, and set it up in the place of the first which had been folded up. All its pillars were new. Its ornaments

---

[F] Jerusalem or the Mount of Olives
[G] Gehenna is a valley immediately south of the city of Jerusalem.

were new and larger than those of the first, which He had removed, and all the sheep in the midst of it.

## Sheep and Goat Judgment

[30]I saw all the sheep which had been left, and all the beasts on the earth, and all the birds of the heaven, falling down and doing homage to those sheep and making petition to and obeying them in everything.

[31]Thereafter, those three who were clothed in white and had seized me [Enoch] by my hand and taken me up before, and the hand of that ram [Elijah] also seizing hold of me, they took me up and set me down in the midst of those sheep before the judgment took place.[H] [32]Those sheep were all white, and their wool was abundant and clean. [33]All that had been destroyed and dispersed, and all the beasts of the field, and all the birds of the heaven, assembled in that house, and the Lord of the sheep rejoiced with great joy because they were all good and had returned to His house.

[34]I watched till they laid down that sword, which had been given to the sheep, and they brought it back into the house, and it was sealed before the presence of the Lord[I], and all the sheep were invited into that house, but it held them not. [35]The eyes of them all were opened, and they

---

[H] Tertullian thought this meant Enoch and Elijah would be the two witnesses of Revelation 11:3.

[I] And He shall judge among the nations, and shall rebuke many people: and they shall beat their swords into plowshares, and their spears into pruning hooks: nation shall not lift up sword against nation, neither shall they learn war any more. *Isaiah 2:4*

saw the Good One, and there was not one among them that did not see. [36]And I saw that that house was large and broad and very full. [37]I saw a white bull [Messiah] that had been born[J] with large horns and all the beasts of the field and all the birds of the air feared Him and made petition to Him all the time.

[38]I saw till all their generations were transformed, and they all became white bulls; and the first among them became a Word, and that Word[K] became a great animal and had great black horns on its head; and the Lord of the sheep rejoiced over it and over all the cattle.

[39]I slept in their midst; and I awoke and saw everything. [40]This is the vision which I saw while I slept, and I awoke and blessed the Lord of righteousness and gave Him glory. [41]Then I wept and my tears flowed on account of what I had seen; for everything will come to pass and be fulfilled, and all the deeds of men in their order were shown to me. [42]On that night I remembered the first dream, and because of it I wept and was troubled because I had seen that vision.

---

[J] Birth of the Messianic Kingdom

[K] In the beginning was the Word, and the Word was with God, and the Word was God. *John 1:1*

# Apocalypse of Weeks 91-93

[Somehow the second half of chapter 93 was placed at the end of chapter 91. We have kept the chapter and verse divisions and simply moved that section back into its original place.]

**91** Now, my son Methuselah, call all of your brothers and all of your mother's children to me; for the Word calls me and the Spirit is poured out upon me, that I may tell you everything that will happen to you in the future. [2]Methuselah went and summoned all his brothers and assembled his relatives. [3]And he spoke of righteousness to all the children. He said, "Listen, my children, to all the words of your father, and take seriously my speech; for I need to warn you, beloved. Love righteousness and walk in it. [4]Do not approach righteousness with a double heart, and associate not with those of a double heart, but walk in justice, my sons. It will guide you on good paths, and righteousness will be your companion.

## Flood Judgment

[5]For I know that violence must increase on the earth and a great judgment will be executed on the earth. All unrighteousness will cease and be cut off at its roots, and its whole structure destroyed.

## Fire Judgment

[6]And unrighteousness will a second time be consummated on the earth, and all the deeds of sin, violence, and godlessness will prevail. [7]When sin, blasphemy,

unrighteousness, and all kinds of violent deeds increase, and apostasy, transgression, and uncleanness increase, there will be a great judgment from heaven upon all these. The Holy Lord will come forth with wrath and judgment to punish the earth. ⁸In those days violence will be cut off from its roots, and the roots of unrighteousness, together with deceit, will be destroyed from under heaven. ⁹And all the idols[A] of the heathen will be abandoned, the temples burned with fire, and they will be removed from the whole earth. The heathen will be cast into the judgment of eternal fire. ¹⁰The righteous will arise from their sleep [resurrection], and wisdom will arise and be given unto them. ¹¹After that, the roots of unrighteousness will be cut off and the sinners will be destroyed by the sword. Blasphemers will be cut off from every place and those who plan violence and blasphemy will perish by the sword.

# 92 The Resurrection

This instruction in wisdom was written by Enoch for every man of dignity, judge of the earth, all his children who dwell on the earth, and future generations who practice righteousness and peace. ²Do not let your spirit be troubled on account of the times; for the Holy Great One has appointed days for all things. ³The Righteous One[B] will arise from sleep. He will arise and walk in the paths of righteousness and all His paths and ways will be in eternal goodness and grace. ⁴He will be

---

[A] Literal Hebrew has "pictures" implying that you don't have to use statues to be an idolater.
[B] The Messiah

gracious to the righteous and give them eternal life.[C] And He will give them power so that they will be endowed with goodness and righteousness. They will walk in eternal light. [5]And sin will perish in darkness forever, and will no more be seen from that day forevermore.

## 93 The Ten Weeks Prophecy[D]
After that Enoch began to recount from the books. Enoch said, "I wish to tell you about the children of righteousness [Christians], the elect [Jews] of the world, and the plant of uprightness [the nation of Israel]. I, Enoch, will declare them to you, my sons, as they appeared to me in the heavenly vision, and as I have been told by the word of the holy angels, and have read from the heavenly tablets." [3]Enoch began to recount from the books and said,

### First Week 1-700 AM, 3925-3225 BC
I was born on the seventh day in the first week[E], while justice and righteousness still endured.

### Second Week 701-1400 AM, 3225-2525 BC
[4]After me there will arise in the second week great wickedness, and deceit will spring up.[F] Afterwards will be the first end [the Flood]. Mankind will be saved, but

---

[C] Or eternal righteousness

[D] There will be ten periods of 700 years; a day for a century. AM stands for "Anno Mundi," the year of Creation.

[E] Enoch was born in 622 AM or 3303 BC. The seventh day of the first week would occur between 600 and 700 AM.

[F] The extreme wickedness began in the first week. The result of this wickedness was the Flood, which occurred afterwards (1656 AM or 2269 BC), at the beginning of the third week.

unrighteousness will revive, even though he will make a law[G] for the sinners.

## Third Week 1401-2100 AM, 2525-1825 BC

[5]After that, during the third week,[H] a man [Abraham] will be elected as the plant of righteous judgment, and his posterity will become the plant of righteousness [the nation of Israel] forevermore.

## Fourth Week 2101-2800 AM, 1825-1125 BC

[6]After that, during the fourth week, visions of the holy and righteous [God at Mt. Sinai] will be seen, and a [Mosaic] law[I] for all generations and an enclosure [tabernacle] will be made for them.

## Fifth Week 2801-3500 AM, 1125-425 BC

[7]After that, during the fifth week, the house[J] of dominion [Solomon's Temple] will be built, forever glorified.

## Sixth Week 3501-4200 AM, 425 BC - AD 275

[8]After that, in the sixth week, all who live in it will be blinded, and their hearts will godlessly forsake wisdom. In it a Man [Jesus] will ascend[K]; and at its close the house of dominion [Herod's temple] will be burnt with fire, and

---

[G] The Seven Noahide Laws. See *Ancient Post-Flood History* pp. 48-50.

[H] God made His covenant with Abraham when he was seventy years old (2018 AM or 1907 BC).

[I] The Mosaic Law was given with a court or tabernacle in 2448 AM or 1477 BC.

[J] Solomon's temple dedicated in 2935 AM or 990 BC.

[K] Jesus ascension was 3957 AM or AD 32

the whole race of the chosen root [Israel] will be dispersed.[L]

## Seventh Week 4201-4900 AM, AD 275-975

[9]After that, in the seventh week, an apostate generation will arise; their rebellion will manifest in many different ways.[M] [10]At its close, the elect righteous [Jewish believers] of the eternal plant of righteousness will be rewarded with a sevenfold instruction[N] concerning all His creation.

## God's Omniscience

[11]Who is there of all the children of men who is able to hear the voice of the Holy One with trembling? Who can think His thoughts, or who is there that can behold all the works of heaven? [12]Who could behold the heaven, understand the things of heaven, see His soul and Spirit and relate to it, or ascend and see all their ends and think and do like them? [13]Who is the man who could know what is the breadth and the length of the earth, and to whom has been shown the measure of all of them? [14]Or is there anyone who could discern the length and height of heaven, what it is founded upon, or could number the stars[O], and know where all the luminaries rest?

---

[L] Temple burnt in 3995 AM or AD 70; Roman dispersion of Israel occurred in 4057 AM or AD 132, after the rebellion led by Simon bar Kokhba.

[M] The anti-Messiah and occultic-type teachings that are found in the Talmud, Gemara, Kabala, and the corruption of the medieval church.

[N] Advancements in science begin to come from the Jewish people sevenfold, compared to Gentiles.

[O] Job 38-39

# 91b Eighth Week 4901-5600 AM, AD 975-1675

[12]After that there will be another, the eighth week, that of righteousness, and a sword will be given to it so it will pass righteous judgment on the oppressors. And sinners will be delivered into the hands of the righteous. [13]During its completion they will acquire houses through their righteousness, and a house [Protestant Reformation[P]] will be built for honor for the Great King forever.

## Ninth Week 5601-6300 AM, AD 1675-2375

[14]After that, in the ninth week, the righteous judgment will be revealed to the whole world [re-establishment of the nation of Israel], and all the works of the godless will vanish from the earth, and the world will be written down for destruction [Great Tribulation], and all men will look to the path of integrity [beginning of the Millennium].

## Tenth Week 6301-7000 AM, AD 2375-3075

[15]After this, in the tenth week, in the seventh part[Q], there will be the great eternal judgment[R], in which He will judge the Watchers[S]. The great eternal heavens will

---

[P] During this time the Protestants took over many Catholic churches and destroyed the idols in them. These churches became their houses of worship. Also this is the time of the creation of the Geneva and King James Bibles in the common language of the people.

[Q] The seventh part is the last 100 years of the 700 year period. This will be between AD 2975 and 3075.
   If the millennium ends with this Great White Throne judgment, then the Second Coming should occur between AD 1975 and 2075.

[R] Great White Throne Judgment at the end of the Millennium. See also Revelation 20:7-9; 21:1.

[S] May refer to Satan's last rebellion; Revelation 20:7-9

appear from the midst of the angels. <sup>16</sup>The first heaven will depart and pass away, and a new heaven will appear<sup>T</sup>, and all the powers of the heavens will give sevenfold light forever.

## Eternity

<sup>17</sup>After that there will be many weeks without number forever, and all will be in goodness and righteousness, and sin will no more be mentioned forever.

<sup>18</sup>Now I tell you, my sons, and show you the paths of righteousness and the paths of violence. I will show them to you again that you may know what will come to pass. <sup>19</sup>And now, listen to me, my sons, walk in the paths of righteousness, not in the paths of violence; for all who walk in the paths of unrighteousness will perish forever."

---

<sup>T</sup> And I saw a new heaven and a new earth: for the first heaven and the first earth were passed away; and there was no more sea. *Revelation 21:1*

# Woe to Sinners 94-105

**94** Now I say unto you, my sons, love righteousness and walk in it; for the paths of righteousness are worthy to be accepted, but the paths of unrighteousness will suddenly be destroyed and vanish. [2]And to certain men of a future generation, the paths of violence and death will be revealed, and they will withdraw from them, refusing to follow them.

[3]Now I say unto the righteous: do not walk in the paths of wickedness and death. Do not even consider them, lest you be destroyed. [4]Choose for yourselves righteousness and a quiet life, walk in the paths of peace, so you will live and prosper. [5]Hold my words securely in your thoughts. Do not let them be erased from your hearts; for I know that sinners will tempt men and make wisdom wicked. No place will be found for wisdom, because all kinds of temptations will increase.

[6]Woe to those who build unrighteousness by violence on a foundation of deceit; for they will be suddenly overthrown, and they will have no peace. [7]Woe to those who build their houses with sin. All their foundations will be overthrown, and they will fall by the sword. The gold and silver they acquired will suddenly perish. [8]Woe to you rich[A], for you have trusted in your riches, but your riches will depart from you, because you did not

---

[A] Compare to James 5:1-8

remember the Most High when you were rich. [9]You have committed blasphemy and unrighteousness; be prepared for the day of slaughter, the day of darkness and great judgment. [10]I declare unto you this: He who created you will destroy you from your foundation. Over your fall there will be no forgiveness, and your Creator will rejoice at your destruction. [11]In those days your righteous ones will be a reproach to the sinners and the godless.

95 Oh that my eyes were a cloud of waters so I could weep over you, and pour out my tears as a cloud of waters, so I might rest from my sorrow of heart! [2]Who has permitted you to practice hate and wickedness? Judgment will overtake you, sinners! [3]Do not fear sinners, you righteous; for the Lord will deliver them into your hands again, that you may pass judgment upon them as you desire. [4]Woe to you who pronounce curses which cannot be reversed; healing will therefore be far from you because of your sins. [5]Woe to you who repay your neighbour with evil, for you will be repaid according to your works. [6]Woe to you, lying witnesses, and to those who weigh out injustice, for you will suddenly perish. [7]Woe to you sinners, who persecute the righteous, for you will be delivered up and persecuted because of injustice, and heavy will be its yoke upon you.

96 **The Rapture and Tribulation**
Be hopeful, you righteous, for the sinners will suddenly perish before you, and you will have lordship over them according to your desires. [2]In the day of the tribulation of the sinners, your children will mount and

149

rise as eagles, and higher than the hawk's nest you will ascend.[B] The sinners will enter the crevices of the earth, and the clefts of the rock[C] forever as coneys. The unrighteous will cry because of you and weep like sirens.[D] [3]Fear not, you who have suffered, for healing will be your portion, and a bright light will enlighten you, and the voice of rest you will hear from heaven.

[4]Woe unto you, you sinners, for your riches make you appear like the righteous, but your hearts convict you of being sinners, and this word will be a testimony against you for a memorial of your wicked deeds. [5]Woe to you who devour the finest of the wheat, drink wine in large bowls, and tread underfoot the lowly with your strength. [6]Woe to you who drink water from every fountain, for suddenly you will dry up and wither away, because you have forsaken the fountain of life.[E] [7]Woe to you who practice unrighteousness, deceit, and blasphemy; it will be an evil memorial against you. [8]Woe to you mighty, who by your might oppress the righteous, for the day of your destruction is coming. Many and good days will come to the righteous in the day of your judgment.

---

[B] The Rapture

[C] And the kings of the earth, and the great men, and the rich men, and the chief captains, and the mighty men, and every bondman, and every free man, hid themselves in the dens and in the rocks of the mountains; *Revelation 6:15*

[D] Satyrs or demons.

[E] For My people have committed two evils; they have forsaken Me the fountain of living waters, and hewed them out cisterns, broken cisterns, that can hold no water. *Jeremiah 2:13*; I am Alpha and Omega, the beginning and the end. I will give unto him that is athirst of the fountain of the water of life freely. *Revelation 21:6*

**97** Believe me, you righteous, the sinners will come to shame and perish in the day of unrighteousness. [2] Be it known unto you sinners that the Most High is mindful of your destruction; and the angels of heaven rejoice over it. [3] What will you sinners do, where will you flee on that day of judgment, when you hear the voice of the prayer of the righteous? [4] You will fare like them against whom this word is a testimony, "You have been companions of sinners."

[5] In those days the prayer of the righteous will reach the Lord, and the days of your judgment will come. [6] All your unrighteous deeds will be read out before the Great Holy One, and your faces will be covered with shame; and He will reject every work which is grounded on unrighteousness. [7] Woe to you sinners, whether you are in the midst of the ocean or on the dry land, your evil will be remembered against you!

[8] Woe to you who acquire silver and gold unjustly and say, "We have become rich, have treasures, and have everything we ever desired. [9] Now we will do whatever we want, for we are full of silver, treasure, and the number of our slaves is as the water." [10] Like water your lies will float away, for your wealth will not abide with you but will suddenly depart from you; because you have acquired it all unjustly; and you will be given over to a great curse.

**98** Now I swear unto you, both the wise and the foolish, for you will have many experiences on the earth. [2] Men will put on more ornaments than a woman, more colored garments than a virgin. In royalty, grandeur, power, silver, gold, purple, in splendour, and in food they will be poured out as water. ³Therefore, they will have no knowledge or wisdom, and they will perish along with their possessions, their glory, and their splendor. In shame, slaughter, and great poverty, their spirits will be cast into the furnace of fire.

⁴I swear to you sinners, just as a mountain does not become a slave, nor a hill become the handmaid of a woman, even so sin was never sent upon the earth. Man of himself created it, and those who commit it will fall under a great curse. ⁵Barrenness was not created for women, but it is by the deeds of her own hands she dies without children.ᶠ ⁶I swear to you sinners, by the Holy Great One, that all your evil deeds are revealed in the heavens,ᴳ and that none of your deeds of violence are covered and hidden. ⁷Do not fool yourself into thinking that no one sees what you do; every sin is daily recorded in heaven in the presence of the Most High. ⁸From now on you know that all the violence you commit is recorded every day till the day of your judgment.

⁹Woe to you fools! Your foolishness will destroy you. Because you do not listen to the wise, you will never obtain anything good! ¹⁰Now you know that you sinners are destined for the day of destruction. Do not even hope

---

F  Abortion was created in pre-flood times. See Jasher 2:18-22
G  For the wrath of God is revealed from heaven against all ungodliness and unrighteousness of men, who hold the truth in unrighteousness; *Romans 1:18*

to live; you will depart and die! There is no ransom for you; for you are destined for the great judgment day, for the day of tribulation and great shame for your spirits.

[11]Woe to you, hard of heart, who do evil and eat blood![H] Where do you get good things to eat, drink, and be filled? All the good things are from the Lord, the Most High, who has made them abundant on the earth; therefore you will have no peace.

[12]Woe to you who love to work unrighteousness! Why do you hope for good for yourselves? You know that you will be delivered into the hands of the righteous, and they will cut off your necks and slay you, and show you no mercy.

[13]Woe to you who rejoice when the righteous have troubles, for no grave will be dug for you. [14]Woe to you who ignore the words of the righteous, for you will have no hope of life. [15]Woe to you who write down lying and godless words, for they write down their lies so that men may hear them and refuse to repent of their foolishness. Therefore they will have no peace, but die a sudden death.

# 99 Bible Corruption

Woe to you godless, who glory in lying and extol liars! Your life will be an unhappy one; then you will perish. [2]Woe to them who pervert the words[I] of righteousness, transgress the eternal law, and try to

---

[H] Eating blood is forbidden in Genesis 9:3-6
[I] They create corrupt Bibles so they can continue in sin.

transform themselves into what they were not, namely sinless[J]. They will be trodden under foot upon the earth. [3]In those days the righteous will ready themselves and raise memorial prayers, as a testimony before the angels, so that they may place the sin of the sinners for a memorial before the Most High. [4]In those days the nations will be stirred up, and the families of the nations will arise on the day of destruction.

## Abortion

[5]And in those days the destitute will abort[K] and mangle their own children, and they will abandon them, so that their children will perish through them. They will abandon their infants, and not return to them, and will have no pity on their beloved ones. [6]Again I swear to you sinners, that sin is prepared for a day of unceasing bloodshed.

## Demonic Idolatry

[7]Those who worship graven images of gold, silver, wood, stone, and clay, and those who worship impure spirits and demons and all kinds of idols,[L] not according to knowledge, will get no manner of help from them [idols and demons]. [8]But they will become godless from the folly of their hearts, and their eyes will be blinded through the fear of their hearts and through visions in their dreams [meditative sorcery]. [9]Through these they will become godless and fearful; for they will have done all their work

---

[J] And no marvel; for Satan himself is transformed into an angel of light. *2 Corinthians 11:14*

[K] Abortion: Jasher 2:18-22

[L] Including saints and angels.

based on a lie, and will have worshiped stones. Therefore they will perish in an instant.

## Salvation for the Righteous

[10]But in those days blessed are all they who accept the words of wisdom, and understand them, and walk the paths of the Most High, and in His righteousness, and do not become godless with all those who act godless, for they will be saved.

[11]Woe to you who spread evil to your neighbours, for you will be slain in Sheol. [12]Woe to you who make a foundation for sin and deception, and who cause bitterness on the earth, for thereby you will reach your end. [13]Woe to you who build your houses through the grievous toil of others, and all their building materials are the bricks and stones of sin. I tell you, you will have no peace. [14]Woe to them who reject the measure and eternal heritage of their fathers, whose souls follow after idols, for they will have no rest. [15]Woe to them who work unrighteousness and help oppression and slay their neighbours until the day of the great judgment. [16]For He will cast down your glory, and bring affliction on your hearts, and will arouse His fierce indignation, and destroy you all with the sword; and all the holy and righteous will remember your sins.

# 100 The Great Tribulation

And in those days in one place the fathers together with their sons will be slain, and brothers one with another will fall in death, till the streams of their blood flow. [2]For a man will not withhold his hand from slaying his sons and his sons' sons, and the sinner will not withhold his hand from his honoured brother. From dawn till dusk they will slay one another. [3]And the horse will walk up to the breast in the blood of sinners[M], and the chariot will sink to its height.

[4]In those days the angels will descend into the secret places, and gather together into one place all those who aided sin, and the Most High will arise on that day to pass great judgment on all the sinners.

[5]But over all the righteous and holy He will appoint His holy angels as guardians to guard them as the apple of His eye,[N] until He makes an end of all wickedness and sin, and though the righteous sleep a long sleep, they have nought to fear.[O] [6]Then the wise children of the earth will see the truth and understand all the words of this book and recognize that their riches will not be able to save them from the overthrow of their sins.

[7]Woe to you sinners, if you afflict the righteous on the day of great travail, and burn them with fire. You will be repaid according to your works. [8]Woe to you, hard hearted, who watch in order to devise wickedness. Fear will come upon you, and there will be none to help you.

---

[M] Battle of Armageddon, Revelation 14:20

[N] The remnant who flee to Petra. "For thus saith the LORD of hosts; After the glory hath he sent me unto the nations which spoiled you: for he that toucheth you toucheth the apple of his eye." *Zechariah 2:8*

[O] Because of the Rapture and Resurrection.

[9]Woe to you sinners, on account of the words of your mouth, and the deeds of your hands which you have done. You godless ones will burn in a pool of blazing flames.[P] [10]Now know that the angels will inquire as to your sins from the sun, moon, and stars[Q] of heaven because you passed judgment on the righteous on the earth. [11]And He will testify against you as to every cloud, mist, dew, and rain that He withheld from you because of your sin. [12]And how you gave presents, not to Him in repentance, but to the rain and dew that was withheld, and to your gold and silver [idols] that it may descend.

## End Time Weather Patterns

[13]In the days when the extremely cold hoar-frost, snow, and all the snow-storms[R] with all their plagues come upon you, you will not be able to stand before them.

**101** Observe the heaven, children of heaven, and the works of the Most High, and fear Him; and work no evil in His presence. [2]If He closes the windows of heaven, and withholds the rain and dew from descending on the earth on your account, what will you do then? [3]If He sends His anger upon you because of your deeds, you cannot petition Him; for you have proudly and insolently spoken against His righteousness. Therefore you will have no peace.

---

[P] Lake of Fire
[Q] Record when you committed each sin. "Sun, moon, and stars" are a reference for the calendar.
[R] Future snow and ice judgments.

157

[4]Do you not see the sailors of the ships, how their ships are tossed to and fro by the waves, and are shaken by the winds, and are troubled? [5]They are afraid because all their good treasures go into the sea with them, and their hearts are fearful that the sea will swallow them and they will perish in it. [6]Is not the entire sea and all its waters and movements a work of the Most High, and has He not set limits to its doings, and bound it by the sand? [7]It dries up at His command, and all its fish die, and all that is in it; but you sinners that are on the earth do not fear Him. [8]Did He not make the heaven and the earth, and all that is in them? Who has given understanding and wisdom to everything that moves on the earth and in the sea? [9]Do not the sailors of the ships fear the sea? Yet sinners fear not the Most High.

102 In those days when He brings a grievous fire upon you, where will you flee, and where will you find deliverance? When He brings forth His Word against you, will you not be afraid? [2]All the luminaries will be greatly afraid; and all the earth will tremble and quake. [3]All the angels will execute their commands and the children of earth will tremble and quake and will seek to hide themselves from the presence of the Great Glory; and you sinners will be cursed forever, and will have no peace. [4]You righteous souls, fear not; hope for the day of your death in righteousness. [5]And grieve not if your soul descended into Sheol, and that your bodies did not find it in your life as your goodness deserved; but wait for the day of the judgment of sinners, and for the day of the curse and punishment.

[6]Yet when you die the sinners say, "As we die, so the righteous die; what benefit do their deeds do for them? [7]Just like us, they die in grief and darkness, and what advantage do they have over us? We are all equal. [8]What is their eternal reward? Behold, they are dead, and they will never see the light of day again."

[9]I tell you sinners, you are content to eat, drink, rob, and sin, and strip men naked, and acquire wealth and see good days. [10]You have seen how the righteous die in peace, because no violence is found in them till their death. [11]Nevertheless, you will perish and become as through you had not been, and your spirits will descend into the grave[S] in tribulation.

# 103 The Mystery of the Resurrection

Now I swear to you righteous, I swear to you by His great glory, honor, and kingdom. [2]I will show you a mystery[T] that I have read in the heavenly tablets, seen in the holy books, and found written and inscribed regarding the holy ones: [3]that all goodness, joy, and glory are prepared for them, and written down for the righteous spirits who have died, and that much good will be given to you as a reward for your labor, and that your lot is better than the lot of the living. [4]The spirits of you who have died in righteousness will live and rejoice. They will

---

[S] Sheol

[T] Paul's mystery - Behold, I shew you a mystery; we shall not all sleep, but we shall all be changed, in a moment, in the twinkling of an eye, at the last trump: for the trumpet shall sound, and the dead shall be raised incorruptible, and we shall be changed.
*1 Corinthians 15:51-52*

be memorialized by the Great One throughout all generations of the world. Therefore, do not fear the shame the sinner will have.

[5]Woe to you sinners, if you die in your sins, and those who are like you say regarding you, "Blessed are the sinners. They have seen all their days. [6]They have died in wealth and in prosperity, and have not seen tribulation or murder in their life. They have died in honor, and judgment has not been passed on them during their life." [7]Know that their wretched souls will be made to descend into Sheol and will be in great tribulation. [8]In darkness, chains, and burning flame their spirits will burn at the great judgment. All the generations of the world will stand in this judgment. Woe to you, for you will have no peace.

[9]Say not in regard to the righteous and good who are in life, "In our troubled days we worked very hard and experienced every trouble,[U] and met much evil and have been injured, and have become few and our spirit weak. [10]We were attacked and found no help; we were incapable in word or deed to accomplish anything. We were tortured, destroyed, and had no hope of survival. [11]We hoped to be the head and not the tail,[V] we slaved away, but had no gain; we became food for sinners and the unrighteous laid their yoke heavily upon us. [12]Those who became our rulers hated us and beat us. We bowed our necks to those who hate us but we received no pity. [13]We

---

[U] The excuse that they had to sin in order to survive.
[V] Deut. 28:13,44; Isaiah 9:14,15

tried to escape from them and find rest, but found no place to flee to be safe from them. [14]We complained to the rulers in our tribulation, and cried out against those who devoured us; but they did not attend to our cries and would not listen to our voice. [15]They helped those who robbed us and devoured us and those who made us few; and they hid their oppression, and they did not remove the yoke of those who devoured us, dispersed us, and murdered us, but they hid their murder, and refused to acknowledge that they had lifted up their hands against us."

# 104

[1]I swear unto you righteous, that in heaven the angels record your goodness and your names are written before the glory of the Great One. [2]Be hopeful, for at first you were disgraced through evil and affliction, but now you will shine as the stars of heaven, and be seen, and the portals of heaven will be opened to you. [3]Continue to cry for judgment. It will appear to you, for all your tribulation will be visited on the rulers, and on all who helped those who oppressed you. [4]Be hopeful, and do not abandon your hopes, for you will have great joy like the angels of heaven. [5]Since this joy will be yours, you will not have to hide on the day of the great judgment because you will not be found as sinners, and the eternal judgment will be far from you for all the generations of the world. [6]Now fear not, you righteous, when you see the sinners growing strong and prospering in their ways. Do not be companions with them, but keep far from their violence; for you will become companions of the hosts of heaven.

[7]Although you sinners say, "All our sins will not be searched out and be written down," nevertheless, they will write down all your sins every day. [8]All your sins will be manifest whether in light or darkness, day or night. [9]Do not be godless in your hearts, nor lie, nor alter the words of uprightness,[W] nor charge the Holy Great One with lying.[X] Do not glory in your idols; for all your lying and all your godlessness issue not in righteousness, but in great sin.

## Corrupted Bibles and Commentaries Created
[10]Now I know this mystery, that sinners will alter and pervert the words of righteousness in many ways, and will speak wicked words, and lie, and practice great deceits, and write books concerning their words.[Y]

## The Bible and the Book of Enoch
[11]But when they write down truthfully all my words in their languages, and do not change or abridge anything from my words, but write them all down truthfully, all that I first testified concerning them, [12]then, I know another mystery, that books[Z] will be given to the righteous and the wise to become a cause of joy and uprightness and much wisdom. [13]These books will be given to them, and they will believe and rejoice in them; and then all the righteous who have learned the paths of uprightness from them will be rewarded.

---

[W] Do not alter the Scriptures.

[X] By saying the Scripture is not inspired and accurate.

[Y] False doctrine and tampering with Bible translations.

[Z] The 66 books of the Bible would be created as a rule and guide for faith. Notice the Book of Enoch is not included in this set of books.

# 105 Everyone Judged by the Bible

"In those days," says the Lord, "the children of earth will be summoned and a testimony given about the wisdom of them [the books of the Bible][AA]: for they are the guides, and a reward for the whole earth. [2]For I and My Son[BB] will be united with them forever[CC] in the paths of uprightness in their lives; you children of uprightness will have peace. Rejoice in their truth.

---

[AA] Everyone will be judged by the Bible, not the Book of Enoch. This shows Enoch was never supposed to be added to the Canon.

[BB] Jesus, the Messiah; the Second Person of the Trinity.

[CC] The Bible will always be true and never be replaced or destroyed.

# Prophecy of Noah's Birth 106-107

# 106<sup>Lemech's Dream</sup>

**106**<sup>Lemech's Dream</sup>After some time my son Methuselah took a wife for his son Lamech, and she became pregnant by him and bore a son. <sup>2</sup>And his body was white as snow and red as the blooming of a rose, and the hair of his head was white as wool, and his eyes were beautiful. When he opened his eyes, they lit up the whole house like the sun, and the whole house was very bright. <sup>3</sup>And when he was taken from the hands of the midwife, he opened his mouth, and spoke to the Lord of Righteousness. <sup>4</sup>And his father Lamech was afraid of him, and fled, and came to his father Methuselah. <sup>5</sup>And he said unto him: "I have begotten a strange son, unlike a man, but resembling the sons of the angels of heaven; and his nature is different. He is not like us; and his eyes are as the rays of the sun, and his countenance is beautiful. <sup>6</sup>It seems to me that he is not sprung from me but from the angels, and I fear that awful things will happen on the earth in his days.

### Lemech Seeks Enoch's Interpretation

<sup>7</sup>Now, my father, I am here to ask and implore you to go our father, Enoch, and learn the truth from him, for his dwelling-place is with the angels."

<sup>8</sup>And when Methuselah heard the words of his son, he came to me at the ends of the earth; for he had heard that I was there, and he cried aloud, and I heard his voice and I

came to him. And I said unto him, "Behold, here am I, my son, Why have you come to me?"

⁹And he answered and said, "I have come to you because of a disturbing vision which has caused me great anxiety. ¹⁰And now, my father, hear me. Unto Lamech my son there was born a son, whose likeness and nature was unlike other men. His color was whiter than snow and redder than the bloom of a rose, and the hair of his head was whiter than white wool, and his eyes were like the rays of the sun, and when he opened his eyes he illuminated the whole house. ¹¹And he arose in the hands of the midwife; he opened his mouth, and spoke to the Lord of heaven. ¹²And his father Lamech was afraid and fled to me, and did not believe that the child was sprung from him, because his likeness was like that of the angels of heaven. And, behold, I have come to you that you may tell me the truth."

## Enoch Interprets the Dream

¹³And I, Enoch, answered and said unto him, "The Lord will do a new thing on the earth, and this I have already seen in a vision. I need to tell you that in the generation of my father Jared, some of the angels of heaven transgressed the word of the Lord. ¹⁴They committed sin and transgressed the law by uniting themselves with women. They committed sin with them, and have married some of them, and have begotten children by them. ¹⁵A great destruction will come over the whole earth, and there will be a flood of water and a great destruction for

one year.[A] [16]This son who was born unto you will be left on the earth; and his three children will be saved with him. When all mankind who are left on the earth will die, he and his sons will be saved. [17]They who begot giants on the earth, not according to the Spirit, but according to the flesh, will suffer a great punishment on the earth, and the earth will be cleansed from all impurity.

[18]And now make known to your son Lamech that he who will be born is truly his son; and call his name Noah. For he will be left to you; and he and his sons will be saved from the destruction which will come upon the earth on account of all the sin and all the unrighteousness, which will be consummated on the earth in his days. [19]And after that there will be still more unrighteousness than that which was first committed on the earth; for I know the mysteries of the holy ones; for He, the Lord, has showed me and informed me, and I have read them in the heavenly tablets.

# 107 The Flood will Not be the Complete End

And I saw written on them that generation upon generation will transgress, till a generation of righteousness arises, and transgression is destroyed and sin disappears from the earth, and all manner of good comes upon it. [2]And now, my son, go and tell your son Lamech that this son, which will be born, really will be his son, and that this is no lie."

---

[A] Genesis 7:11 and 8:14

³And when Methuselah had heard the words of his father Enoch — for he had shown to him everything in secret — he returned with the interpretation and explained it to him and called the name of that son Noah; for he will comfort[B] the earth after all the destruction.

---

[B] Noah means "comfort" in Hebrew.

# Enoch's Last Word 108

**108** Another book which Enoch wrote for his son Methuselah and for those who will come after him, and keep the law in the last days: [2]you who have kept the law and now wait for those days till those who work evil and the power of the transgressors are made an end of. [3]Wait till sin has passed away, for their names will be blotted out of the Book of Life and out of the holy books, and their seed will be destroyed forever, and their spirits will be slain. And they will cry and weep in a void, empty place, and they will burn in unending fire. [4]And I saw there something like an invisible cloud; for by reason of its depth I could not look over, and I saw a flame of fire blazing brightly, and things like shining mountains shaking to and fro. [5]And I asked one of the holy angels who was with me and said unto him, "What is this shining thing? For it is not heaven, but only the flame of a blazing fire, and the voice of weeping and crying and shouting and great pain."

[6]And he said unto me, "This place which you see, it is the place where the spirits of sinners and blasphemers are cast, and of those who work wickedness, and of those who pervert everything that the Lord has spoken through the mouth of the prophets concerning the things that will take place.[A] [7]For some of them are written and inscribed above in the heaven in order that the angels may read

---

[A] Perverting or ignoring prophecy is a serious sin.

them and know what will befall the sinners and the spirits of the humble, and of those who have afflicted their bodies, and been rewarded by God; and of those who have been put to shame by wicked men, [8]who love God and loved neither gold, silver, nor any of the good things which are in the world, but gave over their bodies to torture. [9]Since they came into being, they longed not after earthly food, but regarded everything as a passing breath, and lived accordingly. And the Lord tried them much, and their spirits were found pure, so that they should bless His name. [10]And all the blessings destined for them I have written down in the books: what He has assigned them as their reward, because they have been found to be such as loved heaven more than their life in the world. And though they were trodden down by wicked men, and were abused, reviled, and put to shame, they praised Me.

**Righteous Rewarded with Eternal Glorified Bodies**
[11]And now I will summon the spirits of the good who belong to the generation of light, and I will transform those who were born in darkness, who in the flesh were not rewarded with such honor as their faithfulness deserved. [12]In shining light I will bring forth those who have loved My holy name, and seat each on the throne of his honor.[B] [13]And they will shine for times without number; for righteousness is the judgment of God. For He will be faithful to those faithful in the habitation of righteousness. [14]They will see those who were born in darkness cast into darkness, while the righteous will

---

[B] Matthew 19:28

169

shine. [15]And the sinners will cry aloud and see them shine, and they indeed will go where days and seasons are ordained for them.

Here ends the Vision of Enoch the Prophet. May the benediction of his prayer, and the gift of his appointed period, be with his beloved! Amen.

# Enoch's Prophecies

The main reason most people read Enoch is to learn about the Nephilim. I think the main reason Christians should study Enoch is to learn prophecy. In addition to the many prophecies about Messiah (see the charts in the introduction), there are some very important ones for our time.

In Jewish tradition Elijah is held to be the greatest of all prophets. He formed the school of the prophets to teach those interested in prophecy. In 2 Kings 2 we see his students were called the "sons of the prophets."

The Talmud relates the tradition that Elijah formed the first "school of the prophets" to teach the sons of the prophets how to correctly interpret the prophecies. One of Elijah's basic teachings was that there would be three distinct periods of time: first, the age of Chaos; second, the age of the Torah, or Mosaic Law; and third, the "days of the Messiah."

> "The school of Elijah taught the world is to exist six thousand years. In the first two thousand years was chaos; two thousand years the Torah flourished; and the next two thousand years are the days of Messiah, but through our many iniquities all these years have been lost."
>
> *Talmud, b.Sanhedrin 96a-97b*

171

History shows the Talmud's teaching that each age would last exactly 2,000 years was incorrect. The Years of Chaos were from Creation (3924 BC) to the Exodus from Egypt (1476 BC), a total of 2448 years. The years of Torah were from the Exodus of Egypt to the death of the Messiah (AD 32), or a total of 1509 years. The first two ages totaled 3,957 years. If the days of the Messiah are to be exactly 2,000 years, then they would end before AD 2032. Since the years are off in the first two ages, I do not think the years of each age were taught by Elijah. I suspect Elijah simply taught the concept of the three ages.

Several ancient church fathers taught a seven-thousand-year plan of God. They concluded it was about 4000 years from creation to the death of the Messiah and that there would be a 2000-year Church Age followed by the 1000-year Messianic Kingdom. You can read their opinions and comments from: *Epistle of Barnabas 15:7-9;* Irenaeus' *Against Heresies 5.28;* Hippolytus' *Commentary on Daniel 2.4;* and Commodianus' *Against the Gods of the Heathens 35, 80.*

## Enoch - AD 1975-2075

Elijah probably took his information about the 7000 years from the Book of Enoch, which gives us the same information. In chapters 91-93 is the apocalypse of weeks. It gives us the information that there will be 7000 years of history, followed by eternity. It breaks up the time periods, not in centuries or millennia, but in sets of 700-year-periods. According to this prophecy, the second coming would be in the ninth week, which would be AD

1675-2375. It also tells us that the Great White Throne Judgment occurs in the last day (100 years) of the tenth week, which would be AD 2375-3075. Knowing this is exactly one thousand years after the Second Coming, we can reduce the window to one hundred years, making the Second Coming occur between AD 1975-2075, which fits perfectly within the 700-year window.

### The Shepherds - AD 1948-?
The other end time prophecy we need to consider is the Seventy Shepherds prophecy. In chapter 90 we are told there will be twenty-three rulers (Prime Ministers) ruling a total of fifty-eight times (terms). As of 2012, Benjamin Netanyahu is still Prime Minister of Israel. This leaves us with ten more individual Israeli Prime Ministers who must rule a total of thirty-seven terms or twenty-six more governments. See chapters 89-90 for complete details.

### Jesus' Birth
One completely fulfilled prophecy is given in chapter 10. Seventy generations after Enoch, sin would be atoned for. Luke 3:23-38 records that Jesus Christ was the seventieth generation from Enoch. It is because of Him we may obtain forgiveness and eternal life.

# Appendix A
# The Sons of God (Genesis 6)

Many ask the question "Who are the sons of God in Genesis 6?"

> And it came to pass, when men began to multiply on the face of the earth, and daughters were born unto them, that the sons of God saw the daughters of men that they were fair; and they took them wives of all which they chose. And the LORD said, My Spirit will not always strive with man, for that he also is flesh: yet his days will be an hundred and twenty years. There were giants [Nephilim] in the earth in those days; and also after that, when the sons of God came in unto the daughters of men, and they bare children to them, the same became mighty men which were of old, men of renown.
> *Genesis 6:1-4*

There have been three theories proposed to explain this Scripture. First, the sons are the tyrant rulers of that day and the daughters are just whomever they chose. Second, the sons are the godly line of Seth (Sethites) and the women were the worldly women of the lineage of Cain (Cainites). Third, the sons were angels and the daughters were human women. In this chapter we will look at the possibilities of each theory.

**Tyrant Rulers**
The theory that godly rulers turned into tyrants was proposed by those who took their information only from

the *Ancient Book of Jasher*. Jasher never mentions who these sons of God were, but did say:

> And their judges and rulers went to the daughters of men and took their wives by force from their husbands according to their choice, and the sons of men, in those days, took from the cattle of the earth the beasts of the field, and the fowls of the air, and taught the mixture of the animals of one species with another... *Jasher 4.18*

This is nearly identical with Genesis 6:1-4, but notice that these "rulers" also started experimenting with crossbreeding animals. Where did they get this idea and how did they successfully accomplish this? There is more to the story than to say these "rulers" were just some tyrants.

### Sethites and Cainites

The second theory is the most popular one today. The Cainites were the first to become corrupt and warlike. The posterity of Seth stayed godly long after the Cainites formed, but eventually they also corrupted themselves.

Jewish historian Josephus mentioned the fall of the Cainites who became masters of war.

> Nay, even while Adam was alive, it came to pass that the posterity of Cain became exceeding wicked, every one successively dying, one after another, more wicked than the former. They were intolerable in war... *Josephus 1.2.2*

Josephus also mentioned the fall of the Sethites.

Now this posterity of Seth continued to esteem God as the Lord of the universe, and to have an entire regard to virtue, for seven generations; but in process of time they were perverted, and forsook the practices of their forefathers; and did neither pay those honors to God which were appointed them, nor had they any concern to do justice towards men. But for what degree of zeal they had formerly shown for virtue, they now showed by their actions a double degree of wickedness, whereby they made God to be their enemy. *Josephus 2.3.1*

This presents a few problems:

It is unlikely that a godly peaceful group suddenly turning evil could conquer a race of master warriors, unless you reverse the text and say that the master warriors (Cainites) took over the Sethites and stole their daughters. But the text does not say the sons of men took the daughters of God.

And why is it only ungodly men taking godly women? Why did no ungodly woman marry a godly man and produce a giant?

We are told the children of these matches were giants, but *inbreeding* causes genetic anomalies, but marrying outside of your tribe does not.

**Angels and Humans**
The third theory has been the standard interpretation for centuries. All the ancient rabbis and all the ancient church fathers up to about AD 300 taught the sons of God were angels and the daughters were human women. After AD 200, a movement began to grow denying the sons were angels but rather were Sethites.

In addition to recording the history of the Sethites and Cainites, Josephus also recorded the history of the sons of God of Genesis 6.

> For many angels of God accompanied with women, and begot sons that proved unjust, and despisers of all that was good, on account of the confidence they had in their own strength; for the tradition is, that these men did what resembled the acts of those whom the Grecians call giants or Titans.
> *Josephus Ant. 1.3.1*

Later Josephus mentioned the biblical Amorite giants around Hebron.

> In Hebron there were till then left the race of giants, who had bodies so large, and countenances so entirely different from other men, that they were surprising to the sight, and terrible to the hearing. The bones of these men are still shown to this very day. *Josephus Ant. 5.2.3*

Ancient church fathers who taught the sons of God were angels included: Athinogorius, Clement of Alexandria, Titian, Irenaeus, Tertullian, Myetus of Philippi, Philix, Ambrose of Milan, and Origen.

Church fathers who taught the sons of God were Sethites included: Theodoran, Jerome, Julius Africanus, Chrysostom, John Calvin, and Martin Luther.

If we look carefully at the New Testament we see that Jude quotes from the Book of Enoch (Jude 1:6), which gives an almost complete story of the descent of the two hundred sons of God. Notice that Jude states that God destroyed Sodom and Gomorrah because they committed the same sin as the angels, going after "strange flesh."

> And the angels which kept not their first estate, but left their own habitation, he hath reserved in everlasting chains under darkness unto the judgment of the great day. Even as Sodom and Gomorrah, and the cities about them in like manner, giving themselves over to fornication, and going after strange flesh, are set forth for an example, suffering the vengeance of eternal fire. *Jude 1:6-7*

Those sons of God who went after strange flesh are chained under darkness, according to Jude. Peter says they are imprisoned in hell (KJV). In the Greek, the word for hell is *Tartarus*, also referred to as the bottomless pit in Revelation. Peter says their fall occurred before the Flood.

> For if God spared not the angels that sinned, but cast *them* down to hell [Tartarus], and delivered *them* into chains of darkness, to be reserved unto judgment; And spared not the old world, but saved Noah the eighth *person,* a preacher of righteousness, bringing in the flood upon the world of the ungodly; and turning the cities of Sodom and Gomorrah into ashes condemned *them* with an overthrow, making *them* an ensample unto those that after should live ungodly; *2 Peter 2:4-6*

Scripture refers to angels as "sons of God" and "stars" in Job 1:6; 2:1; 38:7; Deuteronomy 4:19; Isaiah 14:13; Revelation 12:4; 12:9; Genesis 22:17.

Christians are referred to as adopted sons of God in Hosea 1:10; John 1:12; Romans 8:14, 19; Philippians 2:15; and 1 John 3:1-2.

## Conclusion

The consistent teaching of the ancient rabbis and ancient church fathers has always been the sons of God were angels. Genetic problems come from inbreeding, not outbreeding. A pacifist group does not suddenly make their own weapons and take over a group of seasoned warriors. When we take these facts and add to them the fact that Enoch has accurate prophecy fulfilled in our lifetime, the conclusion must be that the sons of God were fallen angels.

# Appendix B
# The History of the Nephilim

Assuming the sons of God in Genesis 6 were angels, we can pull information from the Bible, Josephus, Jasher, Enoch, Jubilees, and other Dead Sea Scrolls and paint a fairly complete picture of the history of the giants.

> And it came to pass, when men began to multiply on the face of the earth, and daughters were born unto them, that the sons of God saw the daughters of men that they were fair; and they took them wives of all which they chose. And the LORD said, My Spirit will not always strive with man, for that he also is flesh: yet his days will be an hundred and twenty years. There were giants [Nephilim] in the earth in those days; and also after that, when the sons of God came in unto the daughters of men, and they bare children to them, the same became mighty men which were of old, men of renown.
> *Genesis 6:1-4*

The Book of Enoch gives a detailed account of the two hundred angels which fell and corrupted all flesh by genetically tampering with animals and mankind. We have seen that these angels married human women. Their children, half angelic and half human, became known as Nephilim. This was an abomination before God. Jude 6-7 states that the angels were bound for committing the same sin that the men of Sodom wanted to do with the angels (Genesis 19:1-5). He then quotes the prophecy in Enoch 1:9. Second Peter 2:4 states these angels are bound in a place called Tartarus (hell in the KJV). According to Enoch 22, this is the special place for holding *only* these angels, their wives, and their sons until the judgment.

For the complete story of the two hundred, see Enoch 6-16. They descended in the days of Jared (460-622 AM; 3465-3303 BC).

> And their judges and rulers went to the daughters of men and took their wives by force from their husbands according to their choice, and the sons of men, in those days, took from the cattle of the earth the beasts of the field, and the fowls of the air, and taught the mixture of the animals of one species with another... *Jasher 4.18*

> For owing to these three things came the flood upon the earth, namely, owing to the fornication wherein the Watchers against the law of their ordinances went a whoring after the daughters of men, and took themselves wives of all which they chose: and they made the beginning of uncleanness. And they begot sons the Naphilim, and they were all unlike, and they devoured one another: and the Giants slew the Naphil, and the Naphil slew the Eljo, and the Eljo mankind, and one man another... And after this they sinned against the beasts and birds...
> *Jubilees 7.18-25*

For many angels of God accompanied with women, and begot sons that proved unjust, and despisers of all that was good, on account of the confidence they had in their own strength; for the tradition is, that these men did what resembled the acts of those whom the Grecians call giants or Titans.
*Josephus Ant. 1.3.1*

In Hebron there were till then left the race of giants, who had bodies so large, and countenances so entirely different from other men, that they were surprising to the sight, and terrible to the hearing. The bones of these men are still shown to this very day. *Josephus Ant. 5.2.3*

Jubilees 10.1-12 informs us that after the flood evil spirits began afflicting many of Noah's descendants. Noah prayed to God to bind all of the demons away from men. God bound nine-tenths of the demons, leaving only one-tenth to tempt and torment man. Revelation 9 tells that the other nine-tenths will be released during the Great Tribulation. If the angels are bound, and the Nephilim are disembodied spirits, where did the giants after the flood come from? A third rebellion? No. The story continues:

Genesis tells us that after the flood Noah divided the planet among his three sons. Ham was given what we call Africa and Shem, the middle east. Canaan, Ham's son, left his territory and ventured North along the Mediterranean Sea. Why did Canaan travel all the way up the cost to found Sidon, his first city, in an area he knew was not his territory, then quickly settle another city (Tyre)?

The map at the right shows that those two locations are the closest he could get to mount an expedition to Mount Hermon. He 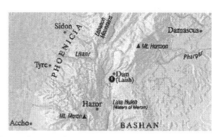 wanted to find information about the pre-flood giants!

> And Canaan grew, and his father taught him writing, and he went to seek for himself a place where he might seize for himself a city. And he found a writing which former (generations) had carved on the rock, and he read what was thereon, and he transcribed it and sinned owing to it; for it contained the teaching of the Watchers in accordance with which they used to observe the omens of the sun and moon and stars in all the signs of heaven. And he wrote it down and said nothing regarding it; for he was afraid to speak to Noah about it lest he should be angry with him on account of it. *Jubilees 8.1-5*

After finding the writing containing the science of the Watchers, Canaan sought to create a race of warrior giants using the same type of genetic tampering which was done before the flood. This explains how the giants came to be, but with a few problems. Second Samuel 21:20 describes giants with six fingers on each hand and six toes

183

on each foot. Moses led the children of Israel into battle with Og, the king of Bashan, who being a true giant, stood at least twelve feet tall (Deuteronomy 3:11). Bashan was anciently called the Land of the Giants. Og actually reigned from Mt. Hermon (Joshua 12:4-5), the place where the angels descended. Even up to King David's time, Goliath remained (1 Samuel 17:4). He was one-quarter giant and three-quarters Philistine and reached only nine feet, nine inches tall. Another race of giants were the Anakim (Numbers 13:21-33). Some of the Amorites were as tall as a cedar tree (Amos 2:9), probably referring to the sons of Anak. Other giant races found in the Old Testament included the Emim (Deuteronomy 2:9-11), and the Zamzummim (Deuteronomy 2:20-21). The Anakim, Emim, and the Zamzaummim were all equally tall. The valley of Hinnom was anciently called the Valley of Giants (Joshua 15:8; 18:16).

Joshua destroyed all the Anakim except for a giant that escaped to Gaza (Joshua 11:21-22), the later home of Goliath. David's men killed Goliath's brother and one other son of the giant (2 Samuel 21:20-21). In four hundred years time the giant out bred, so that Goliath and his brothers were only nine feet tall instead of thirteen feet tall.

The Genesis 6 word for giants (Nephilim) occurs in only one other place: Numbers 13:33. These same post-flood giants who are called *Nephilim* in Numbers, are referred to as *Rephaim* in Deuteronomy 2:11 and Genesis 14:5. These passages show that the post-flood giants were a special kind of Nephilim called Raphaim. This means they were not the procreation of another angelic rebellion, but a genetic tampering by man in a similar fashion as the angels did in the pre-flood world.

## Conclusion

According to the Dead Sea Scrolls, fallen angels procreated the first Nephilim, leading the way to genetic tampering. The post-flood giants were created by this same pre-flood process. The last of the giants were destroyed by the Israelites. See Appendix D to discover how we are heading down that same path today.

# Appendix C
# Book of Giants

The entire Book of Enoch is preserved by the Ethiopic Church and fragments of the same book exist among the Dead Sea Scrolls in the Hebrew and Aramaic languages. There also exist fragments of what is referred to as the *Book of Giants*. These Dead Sea Scroll fragments may prove to be a previously unknown chapter of the story of Enoch. Though very badly fragmented, they provide more details on the practices of the fallen ones.

Dead Sea Scrolls are identified by a sequence of numbers and letters. The first number is the cave in which the scroll was found. The "Q" means it was found at the Qumran site, and the next number is the fragment or scroll number. Compiling the Dead Sea fragments 1Q23; 2Q26; 4Q530, 531, 532; and 6Q8, we come up with part of the original Book of Giants. It is still badly fragmented, so it is an educated guess as to some of the details.

The Book of Giants is made up of two sections.

**Summary of the First Section**
The first section of this work details how the fallen angels descended from heaven and studied all types of creatures from insects to mammals, birds, and even mankind. They took two hundred of each kind of animal or bird and cross

bred them with another kind that had a similar chromosome count to create a creature with an unstable chromosome count. One example given in the text is sheep with 54 chromosomes and goats with 60 chromosomes. This produced a half-sheep, half-goat creature with 56 or 57 chromosomes. Only a few of the two hundred pair combinations would have the ability to reproduce. These unstable life-forms were then crossed with other unstable life-forms with a chromosome count not too different from their own. This process was continued until the desired creature was created. The *Ancient Book of Jasher* mentioned cross breeding cattle with birds. This might have been the origin of the legend of Pegasus, a winged horse. See the appendix on *Genetic Experiments* to see how today's scientists are headed in the same direction.

## Reconstruction of the First Section

When the fallen angels came, they brought great sin upon the earth. Using the secrets of heaven that they knew, they killed many people and animals and they begot giants. *1Q23 Frag. 9, 14, 15*

They studied everything the earth produced, the fruit, grains, and trees, along with the creeping insects up to the great fish, beasts, reptiles, the flying birds. ...every harsh deed ...their oath ...male and female, and among humans... *4Q531 Frag. 3*

They took two hundred donkeys and asses[A], two hundred rams and goats[B], two hundred of the beasts of the field, including various types of animals and birds, for the purpose of mixing species.
*1Q23 Frag. 1, 6*

The angels defiled their women, who begot giants and monsters. The entire earth was corrupted by this blood and by the hand of the giants who devoured much flesh. What the giants did not eat, the monsters attacked. *4Q531 Frag. 2*

The flesh of all the monsters... they would always arise without true understanding and knowledge and the earth grew so corrupt they were considering... from the angels, but in the end it would always perish and die and it caused even greater corruption in the earth... this did not suffice to... said "they will be... *4Q532 Col. 2 Frags. 1 - 6*

According to the books of Enoch and Jubilees, the two hundred angels had children who were called giants. Later, another species was created called the Nephal. The details are sketchy but most scholars seem to suggest the Nephal were the children of the giants, but dramatically inferior to the giants themselves. Later, another species

---

[A] Donkeys which have 62 chromosomes and horses which have 64 produce mules which have 63 and are *almost* always infertile.

[B] Sheep have 54 chromosomes, but goats have 60. When cross mated, they rarely produce surviving offspring. When one does survive, it has either 56 or 57 chromosomes and is infertile.

was created, possibly by mankind. This third species was called Elioud. They were inferior to the Nephal (see notes on chapter 10 for details). The giants were at war with the Nephal and the Nephal hated the Elioud and the Elioud hated and hunted mankind. It is interesting in this second section that the Elioud had dreams of their future destruction and went to get the advice of the giants. No men or Nephal were present. This internal evidence could be a testament to the validity of this text.

**Summary of the Second Section**

The second section gives the account of Mahway, the son of the fallen angel Barakel, who reports a dream of impending doom to his fellow giants. In his dream, he sees a tablet inscribed with many names immersed in water. When it is brought out of the water, it has only three names left on it (a reference to only the three sons of Noah being saved from a world-wide flood). Then Ohya and Hahya, sons of the fallen angel Semyaza, interpret the dream as God's judgment for Azazal corrupting all flesh. The giant Gilga suggests it might be referring to the doom of Azazal and his cohorts, but Ohya describes in his dream that the whole world was a garden that was destroyed by a flood except for three roots of one tree. Then representatives from the Elioud clan come to the giants and relate that two of them had the same dream where two hundred trees in a garden were destroyed by their roots. The Giant Council suggests finding Enoch the Scribe to interpret the dreams. Mahway finds Enoch and the dream is interpreted as a world-wide flood that will destroy all life on the planet.

## Reconstruction of the Second Section

The Watchers immersed the tablet into the water until it was completely submerged, then they lifted it back out of the water... *2Q26*

This vision is one of cursing and sorrow. I decided to bring this before the Council of Gaints. I can still see the spirits of those slain crying out for vengeance, and feel like we will all die together and come to an end because of them. I am afraid to sleep, eat, or even go to my dwelling. What do you think this means? *4Q530 Frag.7*

Ohya was not afraid to ask Mahway, "who showed you this vision, my brother?" ...Barakel my father, was with me. Before Mahway had finished telling... said to him, "Now I have heard wonders! If a barren woman[C] gives birth... *6Q8*

Then Ohya said to Hahya, "all life will be destroyed from the face of the earth when this occurs." And they wept... *4Q530 Frag. 4*

Then Ohya said to Hahya... then he said, "we are not the cause; it is Azaziel, he is the one who... the sons of the angels are the giants, and they would not let all their loved ones to be neglected. ...we have not been cast down; you have strength..."
*4Q530 Frag. 7*

---

[C] After taking the potion and becoming barren, the Lord opened Zillah's womb... *Jasher 2:19-23*

I am a giant and by the mighty strength of my arm and my own great strength I can defeat any mortal. I have made war with them many times; but even I am not able to stand against these opponents, for they are from heaven and they dwell in the holy places. They are not like me; they are much stronger. ...of the wild beast, they call me the wild man. Then Ohya said to him, "I have been forced[D] to have a dream when the sleep of my eyes changed to let me see a vision. Now I know that on the... Gilga..." *4Q531 Frag. 1*

Three of its roots... and while I watched, Watchers came and moved the three roots to another garden,[E] all of them and not... *6Q8 Frag. 2*

These dreams concern the death of our souls; or it may be just the doom of Azaziel and all his cohorts. Then Ohya told them of Gilga's interpretation, that it was for the leader and his cursed cohorts. And the giants were glad at his words. Then he turned and left. *4Q530 Col. 2*

After that two of them had the same dream; and they awoke and came and told their dreams in the assembly of their brothers. The Elioud[F] ... In the

---

[D] Apparently giants didn't normally dream; so when they did, they knew it was a warning.

[E] A dream of a tree destroyed except for three of its roots which are saved by being transplanted into another garden.

[F] Called monsters in some texts

191

dream I was watching this very night, and there was a garden. And gardeners were watering two hundred trees and large shoots came up out of the roots and drained off all the water. And a fire burned up the whole garden. ...We decided to come to the Council of Giants and tell them about the dreams.

Find Enoch, the renowned scribe. He can interpret the dream for us. Then his fellow Ohya spoke and said to the other giants, "I also had a dream last night. In the dream I saw the Ruler of Heaven come down to earth... and then the dream ended." Upon hearing this, all the giants and Elioud grew afraid and called Mahway and pleaded with him to seek out Enoch, the scribe. They said that Enoch can interpret these dreams and tell us how long the giants have to live. *Col. 3*

So Mahway mounted up in the air like an eagle. He left the glen at the edge of the inhabited world and flew over the place of desolation, and through the great desert... Mahway said, "the giants and all the Elioud await your interpretation of the dreams of the two hundred trees that came from heaven, and the other dreams."

Then Enoch the scribe wrote down the interpretation and made a copy in his own handwriting saying, "In the name of the great and holy God to Semyaza and all of his companions. Let it be known to you that because of the things that you and your wives, their sons and their sons' wives have done by your licentiousness on the earth, a sentence has been placed upon you. All of creation is crying out to God and complaining about you and the deeds of your children and the harm you have done to the earth... until Raphael arrives. Behold, a great flood is coming, and it will destroy all living things; all life in the land and sea. This is the meaning of the matter. It will come upon you because of your evil. Therefore, loosen the bonds that bind you to this evil and pray." *4Q530 Frag. 2*

Then I became greatly afraid and fell on my face. I heard his voice and believed him because he dwelt among men but did not practice their ways...

# Appendix D
# Genetic Experiments as of 2012

In 1978 the first report of the birth of a baby from in vitro fertilization came from England. That same year in the US, the National Institutes of Health approved field experiments using altered bacteria.

In 1980 the U. S. Supreme Court ruled that the U. S. Patent and Trademark Office could legally grant a patent on a genetically-engineered "oil-eating" bacteria. Since then, hundreds of patents have been issued on genetically-modified bacteria, viruses, and plants.

In 1988 a patent was granted on a mouse that contained a cancer-predisposing gene. These mice would always develop cancer upon reaching maturity. They are currently used to test cancer-treating drugs.

In 1997 the first sheep and a monkey were cloned. President Bill Clinton then signed a law making it illegal to experiment with, or clone, a human being.

In 2002 Scientists successfully added a gene from a jellyfish to a mouse, creating the first glow-in-the-dark mouse. Later, this was also done successfully on cats, guinea pigs, and monkeys.

In 2008 a mouse that had been frozen for sixteen years was cloned. The clone has reproduced four normal mice. Based on this procedure, scientists are trying to clone a perfectly preserved woolly mammoth found frozen in Siberia, and thereby bring back this extinct animal.

The Pyrenean Ibex became extinct in 2000. It was cloned in 2009, but the clone died nine minutes after birth due to lung damage.

The Dead Sea Scroll, referred to as the Book of Giants, states that the angels experimented with two hundred sets of animals with slightly different chromosome counts. They cross bred them with other genetically unstable life-forms to create whole new species.

In England, the 2008 Human Fertilization Embryology Act was passed allowing researchers to create human-animal hybrid embryos, as long as they were destroyed after fourteen days. This Act was to research how stem cells could possibly cure certain diseases. Over 150 hybrid embryos have been created, both cybrids (human nucleus implanted into an animal cell) and chimeras (animal nucleus implanted into a human cell).

By the year 2012, a process was developed to genetically alter a cow's DNA to produce human antibodies instead of cow antibodies. This was done by taking two strands of human DNA and putting them into a mouse to replicate. At a certain stage of development, these cells are removed and implanted into a chicken, which allows them to be combined in a specific way. They are then removed from the chicken and placed into a hamster. The hamster cell line allows for one last modification, and then it is transferred into the cow after the cow's immune system has been neutralized. The original cow is then cloned. As a result, we can produce an unlimited supply of human antibodies in case of an epidemic outbreak.

## Conclusion

We have begun a spiral to disaster. We are able to bring back extinct species; we have created new bacteria and plants. Now we have begun to create new animal species. We now have glowing mice, cats, and monkeys and partly-human cows that produce human antibodies. Where will it stop?

# Other Books by
# Ken Johnson, Th.D.

### Ancient Post-Flood History

This book is a Christian timeline of ancient post-Flood history based on Bible chronology, the early church fathers, and ancient Jewish and secular history. This can be used as a companion guide in the study of Creation Science. Some questions answered: Who were the Pharaohs in the times of Joseph and Moses? When did the famine of Joseph occur? What Egyptian documents mention these? When did the Exodus take place? When did the Kings of Egypt start being called "Pharaoh" and why? Who was the first king of a united Italy? Who was Zeus and where is he buried? Where did Shem and Ham rule and where are they buried? How large was Nimrod's invasion force that set up the Babylonian Empire, and when did this invasion occur? What is Nimrod's name in Persian documents? How can we use this information to witness to unbelievers?

### Ancient Seder Olam

This 2000-year-old scroll reveals the chronology from Creation through Cyrus' decree that freed the Jews in 536 BC. The *Ancient Seder Olam* uses biblical prophecy to prove its calculations of the timeline. We have used this technique to continue the timeline all the way to the reestablishment of the nation of Israel in AD 1948. Using the Bible and rabbinical tradition, this book shows that the ancient Jews awaited King Messiah to fulfill the prophecy spoken of in Daniel, Chapter 9. The Seder answers many questions about the chronology of the books of Kings and Chronicles. It talks about the coming of Elijah, King Messiah's reign, and the battle of Gog and Magog.

### Ancient Prophecies Revealed

This book details over 500 biblical prophecies in the order they were fulfilled; these include pre-flood times though the First Coming of

Jesus and into the Middle Ages. The heart of this book is the 53 prophecies fulfilled between 1948 and 2008. The last eleven prophecies between 2008 and the Tribulation are also given. All these are documented and interpreted from the Ancient Church Fathers.

The Ancient Church Fathers, including disciples of the twelve apostles, were firmly premillennial, pretribulational, and very pro-Israel.

**Ancient Book of Jasher**

There are thirteen ancient history books mentioned and recommended by the Bible. The Ancient Book of Jasher is the only one of the thirteen that still exists. It is referenced in Joshua 10:13; 2 Samuel 1:18; and 2 Timothy 3:8. This volume contains the entire 91 chapters plus a detailed analysis of the supposed discrepancies, cross-referenced historical accounts, and detailed charts for ease of use. As with any history book, there are typographical errors in the text but with three consecutive timelines running though the histories, it is very easy to arrive at the exact dates of recorded events. It is not surprising that this ancient document confirms the Scripture and the chronology given in the Hebrew version of the Old Testament, once and for all settling the chronology differences between the Hebrew Old Testament and the Greek Septuagint.

**Third Corinthians, Ancient Gnostics and the End of the World**

This little known, 2000-year-old Greek manuscript was used in the first two centuries to combat Gnostic cults. Whether or not it is an authentic copy of the original epistle written by the apostle Paul, it gives an incredible look into the cults that will arise in the Last Days. It contains a prophecy that the same heresies that pervaded the first century church would return before the Second Coming of the Messiah.

**Ancient Paganism, The Sorcery of the Fallen Angels**

Ancient Paganism explores the false religion of the ancient pre-Flood world and its spread into the gentile nations after Noah's Flood. Quotes from the ancient church fathers, rabbis, and the Talmud detail the activities and beliefs of both Canaanite and New Testament era sorcery. This book explores how, according to biblical prophecy, this same sorcery will return before the Second Coming of Jesus Christ to earth. These religious beliefs and practices will invade the end time church and become the basis for the religion of the Antichrist. Wicca, Druidism, Halloween, Yule, meditation, and occultic tools are discussed at length.

## The Rapture

The Pretribulational Rapture of the Church Viewed From the Bible and the Ancient Church This book presents the doctrine of the pretribulational Rapture of the church. Many prophecies are explored with Biblical passages and terms explained. Evidence is presented that proves the first century church believed the End Times would begin with the return of Israel to her ancient homeland, followed by the Tribulation and the Second Coming. More than fifty prophecies have been fulfilled since Israel became a state. Evidence is also given that several ancient rabbis and at least four ancient church fathers taught a pretribulational Rapture. This book also gives many answers to the arguments midtribulationists and posttribulationists use. It is our hope this book will be an indispensable guide for debating the doctrine of the Rapture.

## Ancient Epistle of Barnabas

The Epistle of Barnabas is often quoted by the ancient church fathers. Although not considered inspired Scripture, it was used to combat legalism in the first two centuries AD. Besides explaining why the Laws of Moses are not binding on Christians, the Epistle explains how many of the Old Testament rituals teach typological prophecy. Subjects explored are: Yom Kippur, the Red Heifer ritual, animal sacrifices, circumcision, the Sabbath, Daniel's visions and the end-time ten-nation empire, and the temple.

The underlying theme is the Three-Fold Witness. Barnabas teaches that mature Christians must be able to lead people to the Lord, testify to others about Bible prophecy fulfilled in their lifetimes, and teach creation history and creation science to guard the faith against the false doctrine of evolution. This is one more ancient church document that proves the first century church was premillennial and constantly looking for the Rapture and other prophecies to be fulfilled.

## The Ancient Church Fathers

This book reveals who the disciples of the twelve apostles were and what they taught, from their own writings. It documents the same doctrine was faithfully transmitted to their descendants in the first few centuries and where, when, and by whom, the doctrines began to change. The ancient church fathers make it very easy to know for sure what the complete teachings of Jesus and the twelve apostles were.

You will learn, from their own writings, that the first century disciples taught about the various doctrines that divide our church today. You will learn what was discussed at the seven general councils and why. You will learn who were the cults and cult leaders that began to change doctrine and spread their heresy and how that became to be the standard teaching in the medieval church. A partial list of doctrines discussed in this book are:

| | | |
|---|---|---|
| Abortion | Free will | Purgatory |
| Animals sacrifices | Gnostic cults | Psychology |
| Antichrist | Homosexuality | Reincarnation |
| Arminianism | Idolatry | Replacement theology |
| Bible or tradition | Islam | Roman Catholicism |
| Calvinism | Israel's return | The Sabbath |
| Circumcision | Jewish food laws | Salvation |
| Deity of Jesus Christ | Mary's virginity | Schism of Nepos |
| Demons | Mary's assumption | Sin / Salvation |
| Euthanasia | Meditation | The soul |
| Evolution | The Nicolaitans | Spiritual gifts |
| False gospels | Paganism | Transubstantiation |
| False prophets | Predestination | Yoga |
| Foreknowledge | premillennialism | Women in ministry |

## Ancient Book of Daniel

The ancient Hebrew prophet Daniel lived in the fifth century BC and accurately predicted the history of the nation of Israel from 536 BC to

AD 1948. He also predicted the date of the death of the Messiah to occur in AD 32, the date of the rebirth of the nation of Israel to occur in AD 1948, and the Israeli capture of the Temple Mount to take place in AD 1967! Commentary from the ancient rabbis and the first century church reveals how the messianic rabbis and the disciples of the apostles interpreted his prophecies.

Daniel also indicated where the Antichrist would come from, where he would place his international headquarters, and identified the three rebel nations that will attack him during the first three-and-a-half years of the Tribulation.

### Ancient Epistles of John and Jude

This book provides commentary for the epistles of John and Jude from the ancient church fathers. It gives the history of the struggles of the first century church. You will learn which cults John and Jude were writing about and be able to clearly identify each heresy. You will also learn what meditation and sorcery truly are. At the end of each chapter is a chart contrasting the teaching of the church and that of the Gnostics. Included are master charts of the *doctrine of Christ*, the *commandments of Christ*, and the *teaching of the apostles*.

Learn the major doctrines that all Christians must believe:

| | |
|---|---|
| Jesus is the only Christ | The Rapture |
| Jesus is the only Savior | Creationism |
| Jesus is the only begotten Son of God | Eternal life only by Jesus |
| Jesus is sinless | The sin nature |
| Jesus physically resurrected | Prophecy proves inspiration |
| Jesus will physically return to earth | Idolatry is evil |
| God is not evil | |

### Ancient Messianic Festivals, And The Prophecies They Reveal

The messianic festivals are the Biblical rituals God commanded the ancient Israelites to observe. These ancient rites give great detail on the first coming of the Messiah including the date on which He would arrive, the manner of His death, and the birth of His church. You will also learn of the many disasters that befell the Jews through the centuries on the ninth of Av. The rituals speak of a Natzal, or rapture of believers, and a terrible time called the *Yamin Noraim*. They give a rather complete outline of this seven-year tribulation period, including the rise of a false messiah. They also tell of a time when the earth will be at peace in the Messianic Kingdom. In addition to the seven messianic festivals, you will learn the prophetic outline of other ceremonies like Hanukkah, the new moon ceremony, the wedding ceremony, the ashes of the red heifer, and the ancient origins of Halloween. You will also learn of other prophetical types and shadows mentioned in the Bible.

**Ancient Word of God**
Is there a verse missing from your Bible? Would you like to know why it was removed?

This book covers the history of the transmission of the Bible text through the centuries. It examines and proves, based on fulfilled Bible prophecy, which Greek texts faithfully preserve the ancient Word of God.

You will learn about the first century cults that created their own warped Bibles and of the warnings that the ancient church gave in regard to the pure text. Over two hundred English Bibles are compared. Is the KJV more accurate, maybe the NIV, or perhaps the NASB or ESV?

**Cults and the Trinity**
This book compares Christianity with the false religions of the world today based on the accuracy of fulfilled Bible prophecy. No other religion has used prophecy fulfilled in our lifetime to prove its authority, except the Bible. With more than fifty prophecies fulfilled since AD 1948 and Jesus' teaching that He is the only way to salvation, we can conclude we must be a Christian to gain eternal life.

Jesus declares you must follow His teachings in order to obtain eternal life. Among these teachings is the fact that Jesus is God incarnate, the second person of the Trinity. Numerous church fathers' quotes dating back to the first century AD show this fact as well, and the ancient church defined a cult as a group claiming to be Christian but denying the Trinity.

Listing over one hundred cults and numerous subgroups, this book shows that virtually all of them are nontrinitarians. A detailed, yet simple, study on the Trinity will enable you to witness to all the cults using only this one doctrine.

# Bibliography

Ken Johnson, *Ancient Book of Jasher*, Createspace, 2008

Ken Johnson, *Ancient Paganism*, Createspace, 2009

George Schodde, *Book of Jubilees*, E. J. Goodrich, 1888

John Gill, *A Dissertation Concerning the Antiquity of the Hebrew Language, Letters, Vowel-Points, and Accents*, 1767

R. H. Charles, *The Book of Enoch*, Oxford University Press, 1893

R. H. Charles, *Book of Jubilees*, Clarendon Press, 1913

Ken Johnson, *Ancient Post-Flood History,* Createspace,

Ken Johnson, *Ancient Book of Daniel,* Createspace,

William Whiston, *Works of Flavius Josephus*, Hendrickson Publishers, 1987

Made in the USA
Columbia, SC
21 February 2025

54173049R00113